# Francis Bacon

# Francis Bacon

## FULL FACE AND IN PROFILE

**Michel Leiris**

ARTHUR A. BARTLEY
Publishers
New York & London

*We would like to express our gratitude to Marlborough Fine Art, London, for their valuable co-operation.*

© *Ediciones Polígrafa, S. A.*
Balmes, 54 - 08007 BARCELONA (Spain)

Translation: John Weightman
Reproduction rights: Francis Bacon

I.S.B.N.: 84-343-0514-3
Dep. Legal: B. 41.989 - 1987 (Printed in Spain)

Printed in Spain by La Polígrafa, S. A.
Parets del Vallès (Barcelona)

# CONTENTS

*Ich verlange in allem — Leben, Möglichkeit des Daseins, und dann ist's gut; wir haben dann nicht zu fragen, ob es schön, ob es hässlich ist. Das Gefühl, dass, was geschaffen sei, Leben habe, stehe über diesen beiden und sei das einzige Kriterium in Kunstsachen.*

Georg Büchner, *Lenz.*

*In everything I demand that there should be life, the possibility of existence, and then all is well; we are not then called upon to ask whether the work is beautiful or ugly. The feeling that what has been created has life comes before either consideration and is the only criterion in matters of art.*

## Francis Bacon, full face and in profile

Orestes, only just released from persecution by the Eumenides; Hamlet reassembling his wits after the encounter with the Ghost; Don Juan, no more of a superman than his cowardly valet, but straining every nerve to defy the hell to which the Commander has doomed him; Maldoror, half-angel half-ogre, recovering his breath after the prolonged blasphemy of *Les Chants*; a sort of Falstaff, now jovial now reflective, whose debaucheries have left him looking almost as youthful as when he was a page in the Duke of Norfolk's household; a lucky gambler, directly aware of every aspect of our contemporary upheavals, and whose elegantly modern silhouette we seem to glimpse at that precise moment, wholly outside clock-time, when he stakes his all on a throw of the dice, a hand of cards or the roulette wheel...

Francis Bacon's clean-shaven face, at once chubby and tormented, and as roseate as that of some eighteenth-century English empirical philosopher discoursing over his brandy or his sherry, seems to reflect wide-eyed astonishment as well as an intelligent stubbornness and — allied to a hidden fury — the sensitive distress of a man who has not forgotten that he was once a child whom almost anything could move to wonder.

His forelock, which is well in evidence in all his self-portraits, like a reckless comma staunchly inscribed across his brow, appears to be there as an emblem showing that, inside his head, nothing proceeds according to the lazy norms of some already accepted pattern, but that everything is liable to be called into question, cut short or left in suspense. Perhaps it is this same rejection of ready-made solutions which is indicated by his slightly askew — or, at any rate, not at all full-frontal — stance in many of his photographs; like his walk, always, one might think, on the point of breaking into a dance, it could signify a distaste for the sedate tranquillity of those who have never felt the ground crumbling away beneath their feet.

In contrast to the casual but always irreproachable clothes worn by Bacon, the man (a character irreducible to any single expression) — who, incidentally, should also be seen, with no romantic aura, as the glutton for work he really is, up early every morning, however he may have spent the night before —, the untidiness of his studio, a cluttered mews flat with a permanently littered floor, set in the well-groomed calm of a London residential area, seems, by its very shambles, to call obviously and imperatively for that relative creation of order symbolically represented by the painting of a picture, and, at the same time, to provide for its owner who has allowed so much lumber (painting materials, scattered photographs damaged by neglect, etc.) to accumulate in the place where he habitually sleeps and no less habitually paints, a three-dimensional equivalent of Leonardo da Vinci's famous, and richly suggestive, wall.

Is it not the case that art, whether it gives an account of things as they exist or depends essentially on the play of the imagination, has, as its ultimate function, to save us from disaster by creating, alongside the everyday world, another realm, fashioned according to the requirements of the human spirit and in keeping with an inner order which, by its very nature, is in sharp contrast to the unbelievable muddle of the reality around us? And is there not something comparable between settled, civilized sites, which hold the encircling wilderness at bay thanks to an ordered lay-out of one kind or another, and the plastic arts as creators of images on which the human gaze can fasten, images which, being entities different in essence from the myriad constituents of the external world, provide us, as it were, with points of anchorage? This being so, the artist, once we admit that his activity goes beyond mere entertainment, could be said to find his *raison d'être* in the very existence of the chaos in which we flounder, since, in this confusion, his role is to make his own statement, his own personal statement, tenuous though it may be (and in a truly human voice of a kind that our expressly utilitarian creations cannot echo). Although difficult to describe in respect of his appearance, which is hard to classify within any strict framework, Bacon may, as a painter who insists on being nothing but a painter and less the practitioner of an art than of a ludic activity conveying no message, have an individual tone of voice less resistant to definition.

As if the picture had its own life, and constituted a new reality instead of being a mere simulacrum, an oblique allusion or some appropriately symmetrical pattern (with no more bite to it than a piece of pure ornamentation), that feature in a Bacon canvas which is immediately apprehended and asserts itself unequivocally and independently of any sense of agreement or disagreement — whatever the elements brought into play, and even when the theme of the work puts it on the level of myth rather than of everyday reality — is the kind of *real presence* to which his figures attain, even though this presence has no connection at all with any kind of theology. Through the agency of the figures, the spectator who approaches them with no preconceived ideas, gains direct access to an order of flesh-and-blood reality not unlike the paroxysmal experience provided in everyday life by the physical act of love. And this presence is graced with a wild ambiguity, an alluring iridescence, which makes it a sensuous delight, but one so intense that, despite the attractiveness of its painterly vehicle, to some people, repelled perhaps by its searing impact, it can appear wholly abhorrent.

Far from producing a mere surface excitement or picturesque effect, Bacon's works continue to disturb, to charge — even retrospectively — with good and evil, the always to some extent surprising moment of their initial apprehension, and this is a virtue which bears manifest witness to their exceptional quality. What, after all, is the point of a painting devoid of this ability to obsess, and which, after we have communed with it for some time, seems to be little more than an accident breaking the monotony of the wall against which it hangs? The only works which truly exist and achieve full reality are those which establish a persistent hold over us — as, indeed, can also be the case, since it is quality not duration which matters, with such ephemeral things as a song, an actor's performance or a dance — and influence our subsequent ways of thinking and feeling, instead of simply providing us with an impression, striking and moving no doubt at the time, but which, since it has produced no change in our emotional apprehension of the world, did not carry us beyond the limits of dilettantism.

What Bacon offers in most of his paintings, to whichever phase in his development they may belong, are — leaving aside their purely accessory or decorative elements — depictions of living people or normally banal objects — endowed, or at least apparently so, with a certain figurative veracity directly referential to phenomena experienced through the medium of the senses or, more generally, the sensibility, but about which one can obviously say that, far from being reflections of the surrounding world like those of photography, they result from a completely free use of the technical resources of painting and are likenesses whose nature as painted fictions tends, however, to pass unnoticed, so that they exist more forcefully than any simple representation (they are, it seems to me, entities of a particular type, and not simulacra devoid of independent life). In other words, it could be argued that Bacon's essential aim is not so much to produce a picture that will be an object worth looking at, as to use the canvas as a theatre of operations for the assertion of certain realities. In this respect — although, while making no vain effort to be modern, he undoubtedly belongs to the second half of the twentieth century both through his style and the elements he brings into play — he differs not only from the Surrealists (who, being obsessed with dreams and inventions of a phantasmatical kind, turned their painting into a receptive screen for highly imaginary projections) but also from the Cubists (for whom the validity of painting, as a radical transposition of a motif that was either real or supposed to be so, lay in its strongly structured composition, free of any optical trickery), and again from their great predecessors, the Impressionists (for whom a picture was an open window or a key-hole, flattering the eye with some luminous or filtered fragment of the everyday world).

Avoiding any use of dramatic lighting (since it would incline his work towards a form of Expressionism, whereas he categorically repudiates this tendency, and, as a realist contemptuous of bombastic effects and theatrical or satirical intentions, seeks to translate his sensations in as literal and as persuasive a manner as possible), or of delicate or brilliant visual ingenuities (in the style of the Impressionists), Bacon usually stands the object to be painted in harsh, steady electric light or, occasionally, in clear sunlight unmitigated by anything reminiscent of the weather, so that all is exposed, as it were, to a midday glare — midday being a temporal peak and *the moment of truth* — or in the equivalent of what, in theatrical parlance, is called "lights full up". Can we not, then, conclude from this that, throughout his work, this multifaceted artist insists on putting all his cards on the table and — being equally averse both to shilly-shallying and old-fashioned niceties — pays cash down, as it were, in that "immediacy", which he agrees is characteristic of some of his works, as he explains to the art historian, David Sylvester, in one of their dialogues transcribed from long tape-recordings — there are four dialogues in the 1975 edition, seven in the revised edition of 1980 and an eighth, as yet unpublished — which could be continued indefinitely, given the insistence shown by the two speakers in trying to dispel any ambiguity in relation to the questions discussed — exemplary documents, showing how far removed Bacon is from wishing to maintain any coy reticence about his work and how his apparent untidiness goes hand in hand with a rare intellectual rectitude? An immediacy due, I should say, not only to the suddenness of the effect produced but also to the abrupt challenge with which the spectator finds himself unceremoniously faced, on a par (it would seem) with the artist himself, who is always deeply implicated in his work, just as he can be seen to be directly involved in his unambiguous replies to the implacable questioning of his shrewd and persistent inquisitor.

The space in which we breathe and the time in which we live here and now: this is what we find, almost without exception in Bacon's pictures, which seem to aim at the immediate expression of something immediate, and which cannot be adequately described simply by saying that, in general, they avoid the exotic and the archaic, the only works not respecting this rule being *Landscape with a Rhinoceros* (1952, based on a photograph taken in Equatorial Africa, and in any case one of the canvases later destroyed by the artist, as has happened with many others), *Man Carrying a Child* (1956, a memory of a long stay in Tangier), the *Popes* (1949-1952), inspired by the famous painting of Innocent X by Velázquez, and the portraits of Van Gogh (1957), — some of them slightly Fauvist in treatment — which are anachronistic up to a point, being almost, but not quite, of the present. Between most of Bacon's pictures — in this connection, at least, I would like to emphasize his singularity — and the people looking at them, the proximity is indeed greater than if their themes merely involved no spatial or temporal distancing. Although such pictures have no relationship with *trompe l'œil* (an ersatz by which, in any case, no-one is seriously deceived), and the artist has ensured that they are authentic creations, equally distinct from both abstract and what he pejoratively terms "illustrational" or "illustrative", art, it could be said about them that they make the spectator feel as if he *were there,* or even *is actually there* (inside the picture, not simply in front of it), a form of words which expresses the feeling of total participation and, in this sense, goes further than Roland Barthes' trenchant phrase, *that is,* which he applies to photography in his undeniably illuminating book, *Camera Lucida,* to indicate that the past is replaced by the present: *that was* signifying that the paradoxical function of photography is not so much to offer an immediate and artless representation of phenomena as retrospectively to bear witness, since the process is by definition retrospective, and to assert authoritatively that something has existed or occurred.

In many of Bacon's canvases, those which — according to my admittedly subjective point of view — seem the most typical, in other words, those belonging to the period of full maturity, by which time this self-taught artist had, without benefit of any formal instruction and, as it were, through sheer physical effort, provided himself with a technique, objects are shown to us in a space delineated (approximately) according to the traditional rules of perspective, and are correspondingly convincing. They are quite close to us, apparently life-size, and they seem to rest on a floor which might be an extension of that on which we are standing as we look at the picture. It is as if we were no longer pure spectators, but were actually involved with the objects. In such pictures — which certainly have their own kind of geometry but, as it were, of a peripheral sort (relating only to the marginal areas), and not affecting the figures, which are too freely handled to be reducible to simple structures — the overall construction seems to correspond less to a decorative, or strictly plastic, intention than to the requirements of the total organization, presentation or operativeness of the elements, — both on the part of the artist building up the work and that of the spectator, whose eyes and mind are caught and expressly compelled into participation. Being usually closed and exiguous, the space of the picture — an area which appears to be neither a substitute for our world nor a small-scale model of it, but its actual reflection — seems to constitute — whether it happens to be a featureless room or some outdoor, and invariably banal, space — a kind of box in which, ideally, the spectator himself is included, and thus fictitiously introduced into the very place where the object, apparently on the same scale as himself, is on show for him, and where, having been promoted from the innocent role of a mere armchair observer to that of a *voyeur* fully present at the quasi-anecdotal, but non-summarizable, episode set before him, and trapped in a space more often than not enclosed in itself but still open to him, he can be imaginatively present — to which end, indeed, the whole artistic apparatus seems to have been organized.

The space, then, in which we live, but our time as well. Many of Bacon's works, in addition to containing elements drawn from his personal history (he was a furniture designer for a while, before his vocation as a painter declared itself, more or less, one might say, as painterly qualities declare themselves within the frigid structures of the canvases) are apparently conceived with the intention of making their topicality obvious. Contemporaneousness is a feature of the dress worn by the human figures and of the (invariably functional) furniture they make use of, as well as of the other accessories, all strictly relevant to the present time: electric light-bulbs or switches, rugs, umbrellas, safety-razors, wash-basins and lavatory seats, telephones, cameras, illegible newspapers (their tattered fragments, littering the floor, convey an impression of untidiness analogous to the real untidiness in the artist's studio), half-smoked cigarettes (again as if to emphasize, by reference to a precise moment, the picture's quality of being taken from real life or caught *in flagrante delicto*, like a Joycean epiphany), arrows which seem to be borrowed from traffic-signs or from drawings relating to movement, such as are to be found in technical handbooks, and so on. All this material is dealt with not so much pictorially as in a strictly informative style (with no aestheticization of the industrial object, such as is usual in Fernand Léger's work or, to a greater or lesser extent, in Man Ray's "rayographs"). Just as, by other means, the space of the picture is rendered in terms of our space as spectators, so Bacon seems to be determined clearly to signify that what he is seeking to invest with an appearance of life is situated — as everything authentically alive must by definition be — in a time which can be none other than our own. The clothes (always modern and commonplace) or the nakedness (totally non-classical) of Bacon's characters, might be his or ours at this very moment.

Bacon's painting, while doubly immediate (its effect is immediate and it deals almost always with the here and now), has the further characteristic of conveying no message, as he categorically states in one of his first dialogues with David Sylvester, at the same time as he rightly objects to being too hastily labelled an Expressionist. Is it not obvious that his aim is to practise a form of painting devoid of, as it were, any form of distancing? Art of this kind, just as it excludes remoteness in space or time, cannot tolerate that other sort of non-immediacy which might be called reflective distancing: that which characterizes art requiring an effort of thought for its full, and always to some extent postponed, appreciation, since it proceeds by allusions calling for more or less lengthy interpretation, and its action, far from operating with instantaneous effect, only makes itself felt with some delay, after a roundabout process which obviously diminishes its impact, while perhaps increasing its resonance.

Although, both in its texture and in its iconography, Bacon's painting is not at all austere, it can be said to exemplify a paring down, in the sense that it shows a complete disregard for symbols, or for anything that might suggest associations with folklore or with extraordinary phenomena foreign to our everyday context. A paring down which, in its essence, is comparable to that of games or gambling, as might be expected in the case of someone who is not only a real-life gambler (devoted to roulette, that rapid, and wholly aleatory game of chance), but who also believes that painting, having completely lost its sacralizing function in the modern world, can now be no more than a game (a very debatable view, one must admit, since it disregards the fact that painting can still have an educational role, however misapplied). Can we not say that, like art as Bacon conceives of it (a demystified art, cleansed both of its religious halo and its moral dimension — two aspects which were almost one and the same — and hence profoundly realistic, even in those rarer cases where the habitué of the bar of the late Muriel Belcher, of whom he painted several portraits, makes no attempt to render any external reality but endeavours to make real, to give irrefutable body to, something purely internal and perceptible only to himself), games or gambling — activities with no inherent justification but to which one can nevertheless devote oneself with deadly consequences — are essentially things of the immediate moment, valid in the present (not according to any finality involving subsequent effects), and devoid of any meaning outside their sheer practice?

If, as he maintains, art, in the contemporary world, can be nothing more than a game (a very different concept from that of *art for art's sake,* since it implies no special valorization tending to replace sanctifying art by the sanctification of art itself), how far can it be said that Bacon, with his perfectly secular mind closed to any possibility of transcendence, goes beyond pure entertainment in practising this game, to which he appears to be still more passionately attached than he is to classic games of chance?

Unlike Picasso, that other practitioner of a very great game who seemed to delight in trying out the most diverse methods of conveying meaning and so called into question the whole language of painting, Bacon — very similar in this respect to his contemporary, Alberto Giacometti — appears to have striven to be a figurative artist of the most accurate and effective kind possible. In his case, the game consists not so much in the invention of signs as in the struggle between the artist and what he aims at signifying, a contest which, being the interplay between the contingent nature of the theme and the image the artist makes of it by trusting to his subjective impulses, engenders the "tension" that Bacon is looking for and which, in his opinion, is inevitably lacking in non-figurative works.

Apart from a few large canvases of an undeniably tragic nature, which for the most part take the nowadays unusual form of triptychs, and a small number of works whose themes are borrowed from natural phenomena other than man (animals, one or two landscapes, grass, a jet of water, a sand dune), Bacon's favourite subject is, manifestly, the living reality of human beings. In this connection, it is notable that his work, although quite varied, includes no example of a still-life — if we except *Study for a Figure* (1945-1946), which consists simply of a folded overcoat next to a hat and a pile of flowers, and the half-open travel-bag in the central panel of the 1967 triptych, inspired by, but revealing no visible connection with, T.S. Eliot's "Aristophanic melodrama", *Sweeney Agonistes* — and also notable that even water and sand, when he makes use of them, appear to be inhabited by some violent gushing or swirling movement which gives them a semblance of life, the life that Bacon, whether he is transcribing or inventing, seems to be trying above all to express, instead of attempting to remould and then reconstitute the form or contours of the subject, whether real or imaginary, and thus perhaps endow them with a meaning. In fact, I would go so far as to say that Bacon's most Bacon-like pictures are those which, in their general structure as well as in the treatment of the figures, suggest the rhythm of life. Just as, in the real world, the exceptional moments (in which adventure occurs) stand out against the humdrum nature of ordinary living, so the backgrounds of these pictures — like calm waters — are broken here and there by patches of virulent painting which, in contrast to the coolness of the surrounding *décor,* seem to be like fissures through which the painter's sacred fire, non-domesticated at these points, is burning in total freedom. As one observes him exploiting this opposition between a clearly established order and the disorder within it, one is confirmed in the view that — through artistic intuition more than by any logical process — he must have gradually discovered the necessity of a difference in potential if the current is to flow and to give rise to something resembling life.

In a Bacon canvas, then, there are incandescent parts, seething with energy, in contrast to neutral parts where nothing is happening. The former, which defy rational control and are comparable to what in jazz are called ''breaks'', solos grafted onto the beat of the basic rhythm — i.e., in more classical terms, frenzied or Dionysiac parts contrasting with calm, Apollonian parts — might be thought of, if we bring in a romantic reference to Stéphane Mallarmé, that poet of flame and crystal who used the black-and-white pattern of a typographical lay-out not unlike newspaper headlines to give a lofty metaphysical dimension to a game of absolute chance, as areas where the dice are thrown hurricane-like (where the great game is being played), the other areas being little more than *the undifferentiated neutrality of the abyss,* serving only to constitute the place where certain entities manifest their pictorial presence as if to contradict the formula defining the inane: *nothing will take place but the place.* That place, in this instance, is practically non-existent yet must be perceived as a place (painting being essentially a matter of direct sensory perception). Therefore it demands to be clearly established as a place, although in fact it has little claim to appear, serving as it does merely to house the character, or characters, who give life to the picture, as if it were a sort of abstract annexe of the real place where the work is on exhibition and the spectator is standing, and were there to provide a continuity allowing the latter to gain a foothold in the area containing the opaque density of the figures, which are so close to him, appear contemporaneous with him, and with which he cannot help but identify to some extent.

Given the fact that, on the one hand, the invention of photography relieved painting of any "reporting" function (as Bacon points out), so that it is free to develop its own modes of figuration, while, on the other hand, it is impossible for a painter simply to copy the figure he is dealing with to give an impression of reality because, if he does so, the deception is immediately obvious, recourse must now be had to something other than photographic transcription. The spectator will have a chance of believing in the figure presented only if it bears the living mark of the artist's hand (failing this, no contact will be established), and only if there is some degree of distancing, even though this distancing may be violent enough to give rise to a misunderstanding, so that the profoundly realistic tenor of works such as those of Bacon and his glorious predecessor, Picasso, is explained in terms of Expressionist intentions, whereas, in fact, they contain no caricatural exaggeration relating to what Bacon refers to pejoratively as "illustrational" art, but correspond to a more radical and more difficult ambition, which is to operate a plastic remodelling in depth. Using distortions not motivated by a dramatic, or even a purely aesthetic, intention, Bacon, in painting a figure, seeks to translate a true or fictitious reality about whose immediate and actual existence the spectator will entertain no doubt, once he sees it projected almost life-size onto the canvas as a representation cleansed of all those habitual ways of looking at things which, in the ordinary process of living, prevent us, or almost prevent us, from seeing it — a displaced representation breaking the visual routine which obliterates perception, and yet reminding us of the times and of the setting in which we live; and the artist's practice, in doing so; is something akin to transmutation and, like transmutation, subject to numerous chance effects. Consequently, in more than one instance, there is so severe a distortion of the forms that some admirer of Oscar Wilde might be led to conclude too hastily that, reversing the operation of Dorian Gray's magic portrait, which protected the real-life appearance of the hero by taking his gradual decay entirely upon itself, Bacon's portraits, as if endowed with some prescient power, show their models from the outset as creatures already attacked by decay.

Contrary to what one might be inclined to think, presence — an enigmatic quality, independent of aesthetic systems and resistant to analysis — is not a matter of style: it may be missing from a highly elaborated painting demanding an effort of interpretation and a considerable measure of participation from us, the interchangeable spectators (as if presence, which constitutes the very life of the picture, were nothing other than the presence of the figure composing itself in our minds as spectators, on the basis of the immediate data of perception), but, conversely, it may characterize some almost naturalistic work, whose subject-matter offers no difficulty of apprehension.

In the case of Bacon's pictures — at least those I consider to be most curiously alive, irrespective of any question of quality — their extreme intensity seems to me to result from the paradoxical conjunction of two procedures: a more or less marked distortion of the figures, combined with a fairly naturalistic treatment of their surroundings. Being a surprise factor (in view of its remoteness from what one might reasonably have expected), such a marriage of hot and cold cannot fail to arouse attention and heighten the sensation of presence. But this unlikely union is only one example amongst others of the contradictions characteristic both of Bacon's life and of his artistic practice: in a given picture, the coexistence — which I again emphasize — of large areas treated with apparent indifference (backgrounds in flat tints) and of sections produced by what one might call *pictura picturans,* a form of painting which seems to result from a sudden unleashing of mental, as well as manual, energy (the figures); a relatively geometrical patterning of the setting, the firm arrangement of which stands in opposition to the sometimes almost indefinable form of the figures which, in some cases, seem to lose their bone-structure to become strange fluxes or whorls of matter in fusion; and, in the portraits essentially, the liberties arising from the decision not to be illustrational and the constraints imposed by the determination to arrive at an exact resemblance, in so far as it is possible for the painter to square the circle by rendering his subjective and quasi-arbitrary reaction to what he knows of the character's external appearance without disregarding the public data supplied by photography which, in this instance, is used not as a source of inspiration but as a ''control'' (in the form of photographs of the passport kind, as far removed as possible from the ''artistic'' variety and devoid of anything that might influence the imagination, and serving therefore as mere guide-lines, not as catalysts, as was the case, for instance, with some of Muybridge's work dating from the end of the nineteenth century and dealing with bodily postures and movements, or medical photographs of the insides of mouths such as have often provided Bacon with a documentary starting-point for his work); the wholly secular nature of an art which insists on being nothing more than a game and, with realistic intent, attributes no other role to its themes than to be what they are, whereas, on the formal level, leaving aside the direct references to religious paintings (such as the *Crucifixions* which, for the most part, have no iconographical relationship with the death of Christ but are elaborated in triptych form, as if for the purpose of some edifying ceremonial that has lost its content but kept the pattern of its ritual, just as for James Joyce, Bacon's near-compatriot and near-contemporary, the pattern of the ancient *Odyssey* served as a model for that of his very modern *Ulysses*), — whereas, I say, Bacon's art, at once suitably composed and furiously spontaneous, not only makes great use of a convergence between modernity and tradition (hence its frequent recourse to the eminently classical form of the triptych which, as it were, enfolds the spectator within itself and — so Bacon has told me — was suggested to him by the panoramic screens of certain cinemas) but also, since its cool framework so often seems intended to restrain an almost savage violence, appears to be marked by a surface ritualism at least, just as, on a quite different plane, that of everyday life, the discipline of English good breeding — decorum in private relationships — is, with Bacon, a discipline of pure courtesy, and by no means excludes unruliness or tends to act as a censor of desire.

The distortion is so acute that it borders on disruption and, to say the least, suggests that André Breton's assertion: *beauty will be convulsive or not exist at all* has been raised to the status of a principle demanding absolute obedience, — an alteration of natural forms which may be carried to the point of blurring or even obliteration, — in one way or another a profound upheaval, the disturbing, disconcerting and, for some people, scandalous character of which arises from the fact that when Bacon seeks to convey the feeling of (not to describe) some given or invented reality, and for this purpose resorts to distortion, he does not simply alter the form (in the manner of the Cubists who, in calling so magnificently into question all the traditional means of the language of painting, tended to disregard the materiality of objects in order to concentrate on their outlines) but also the substance of the motif, and in particular the flesh of the model, which is rendered in its very warmth and elasticity, both of these features being indicative of life. Bacon's abrupt departure from a literal representation of the motif with the sole aim of rediscovering it in a more telling form undoubtedly constitutes a more thorough and more real onslaught on the real than if he limited his assault to the structure: the distortion is apprehended all the more strongly as such in that the motif is in no way robbed of its materiality, and moreover is rendered as being expressly immediate (therefore in close proximity to us), and is, in general, accompanied by a comparatively naturalistic respect for perspective in the treatment of the setting and even in the overall definition of the figure.

Not only are Bacon's characters devoid of any psychological dimension, always presented in their substantiality and, when appropriate, clad in some form of dress — set before us, then, in their strictly physical, as well as social, existence — the painter shows himself to be as literally materialistic in his work as might be expected of someone who, in discussing his conception of painting, refers to his "nervous system" rather than his personality, thus demonstrating his refusal to idealize even in his choice of words, and who, besides, makes no use in his work of drawing as such, as if he wished to avoid its abstract unreality and preferred the direct application of paint with the brush or some other means, so as to put himself, as it were, in direct contact with the object: not only remodelling the forms but kneading the very matter itself in the shape of coloured pastes and other ingredients, perhaps the most suitable procedure for someone like Bacon, who wants to reach the deepest level, the substratum, and who, by treating appearances with the greatest freedom, is not so much trying to express the real thing, whether perceived or conceived but in either case interpreted in a largely subjective mode, as seeking to render — if I may so put it — the reality of the thing, its very existence, apprehended (if this were possible) over and above its circumstantial features, so as to keep no more than its biting essence, an essence that Bacon, by paradoxical means, appears to convey with extreme sharpness, through some fluke almost comparable to the isolation of that "cutting" virtue, supposedly held in reserve in as yet

unblunted razor-blades, at least according to a literal accept-
ance of Marcel Duchamp's "pataphysical" humour.

To strip down the thing so as to retain only its naked reality — such, no doubt, is Bacon's aim, although the thing in
question may be only one element among others of the general image of the work in progress (the basis of the effort
to embody the particular image that has occurred to him,
although, during the pursuance of the effort, more often than
not a quite different image will replace the original one), and
although it may, in most cases, be something realistic in spirit
but imaginary, and not a motif borrowed from the external
world, such borrowing being by now very rare in Bacon's
case, since he paints his portraits from memory, with the help
of photographs and without asking his subjects to pose,
the actual presence of the sitter inhibiting him, he says, when
he is submitting the image to the desired distortions (and perhaps, generally speaking, because, for him, contact with the
living reality to be painted is something so poignant that he
cannot contemplate it except through the intermediary
agency of photography). These distortions are necessary audac-
ities since, but for them, the image would be no more than
an effigy, whereas Bacon, thirsting for irrefutable presence,
appears unable to restrict himself to evoking representations of
real or imaginary people or things so as simply to fill the surface of the canvas, but to insist, however arbitrarily they may
be treated, on giving them positive existence in the fictitious
space allotted to them. Since, in his case, sensation, either direct or mediated through photography, takes precedence over
ideation, and since his chief driving-force is a vehement desire
to grasp reality, we can say that Bacon has a frenzied, as well

as an effusive, approach to that reality which, above all others, he is endeavouring to translate, and that this frantic, almost panic, urge produces an emotional breaching of boundaries which introduces, into the texture of the canvas, the disturbance felt by the artist himself, so that it is less through deliberate than through what might be called affective, distancing (often carried so far that the artist appears to be creating figures on the point of overflowing or in a state of liquefaction) that he achieves the sensation of presence, unobtainable otherwise either by a copy or an intellectual transcription.

*"Tentative de capturer l'apparence avec l'ensemble des sensations que cette apparence particulière suscite en moi"* (An attempt to capture the appearance together with the cluster of sensations that the appearance arouses in me): such was Bacon's definition of realism in a letter to me, written in French with the help of a common friend, although in fact he has an excellent command of the language but is always afraid that his knowledge will be inadequate for the precise and totally unambiguous expression of his thought in the kind of rigorous discussion he seems to enjoy. "It may be that realism, in its most profound expression, is always subjective," was another remark in the same letter, following up various conversations we had previously had on the subject, a general concern of mine at the time, and during one of which he had pointed out that there are "inner realities", and that realism in art must not be confused with the simple desire to give a translation, in convincing terms, of objectively existing phenomena.

The motif, whether discovered or imagined — obtained from without or within, selected in broad daylight or wrested from darkness — after being treated by the artist in his role as presenter or fabricator, must give the consumer the feeling of being confronted with a new reality, weightier than an image; such, in my view, is the meaning of realism as understood by Bacon, a realism — comparable to that of Picasso, amongst others — which is not simply transcriptive but creative, is less concerned to represent than to establish reality, and may even, thematically, go beyond the limits of verisimilitude, without however acquiring any tincture of idealisation. It is an extreme kind of art, beautifully exemplified in the overpowering 1982 picture, originally the central panel of a triptych that was later reduced to a single canvas, which shows a male body, a solid mass of flesh, resting on a table the four legs of which are all on the same line, a body reduced to an armless, headless trunk with blatant sexual attributes and crowned with two hillocks in the form of a pulpy, skywards-facing rump, a compact idol which also includes — besides a pair of heavily shod feet — two legs half hidden by cricket-pads, impedimenta which seem to immobilize them like splints and thus, through a kind of antiphrasis, to make them more keenly perceptible as living limbs. It was followed, also during 1982, by its female equivalent (a headless trunk crowned by two breasts, inspired by an Ingres drawing), and by another male torso (richly sculptured but without stiffness, since it is presented in movement, and is not the only as it were ''Futurist'' attempt by Bacon to follow a body in its action).

Not being ''slices of life'' in the manner of the works of the Naturalist school of writers, Bacon's most strictly realistic, but non-anecdotal, pictures are more in the nature of flash photographs comparable to Joycean epiphanies, banalities coinciding so perfectly with their formulation that they are suddenly raised to the level of disturbing presences, as, for instance; the *Dog* coming towards us more or less blindly (1952) or accompanied by its master's shadow (*Man with Dog,* 1953); a young man, whose speed cleaves the air we breathe as, with windswept hair, he rushes forward on his bicycle (*Portrait of George Dyer Riding a Bicycle,* 1966); a woman standing on a pavement, where we also seem to be, while a car goes by on the roadway beyond (*Portrait of Isabel Rawsthorne standing in a street in Soho,* 1967); two replicas of Leopold Bloom, in felt hats, sitting side by side as if for the exchange of probably trivial remarks, but that we feel we might overhear if we so wished (*Two Seated Figures,* 1979).

Although the theme of a Bacon painting is never anecdotal, or at least the power of the painted surface, invariably unenhanced by any eye-catching title, never depends on the actual or supposed event referred to — a homosexual coupling, for instance, or, in a 1971 triptych, a man preparing to ascend a dimly lit staircase, and recognizable as the George Dyer of many other paintings, who had died tragically not long before — we can say that a canvas of this kind is, first and foremost, a space in which something occurs, takes place, or comes into being in a sort of ''happening'' which, in the last analysis, is none other than the revelation of the presence aimed at in all Bacon's works, and without which the overtly manual activity from which it results would remain null and void. More often than not, it is a human presence, but it may also be, so to speak, the elemental presence of a fragment of nature devoid of anything that might resemble a soul: the grassy space forming the motif of the 1978 *Landscape* (reduced, more or less, to a duly circumscribed sample of grass, so that the transcription is given more force through compression), the 1979 jet of water (achieved through an actual projection of liquid), the 1981 sand dune (the result of rubbing or pulverization), and more recently — as the artist himself has told me — water from a running tap. When this presence is the human presence, which seems, throughout his different phases, to remain Bacon's major objective — always falling short of the absoluteness he aims at — he may make use of various devices, quite remote from Expressionism, to produce an oblique intensification, as, for instance, in several canvases or triptychs painted in the sixties and seventies: a shadow taking the eminently material form of a pool or blot that seems to have been secreted by the figure, which thereby acquires greater weight; a reflection, like an appendage or a double with the same density as the original, so that the latter's reality is confirmed by the repetition; the omission of part of the body under consideration or, conversely, its emphasizing through some addition (the Verist painting in of splints or other accessories intended to offset a physical handicap but which, in fact, highlight it more than they conceal it) or, sometimes also, the problematic or even acrobatic positioning of the body in an apparently unbalanced attitude or on the point of falling, and so, one might say, more conscious of itself and therefore more telling in its effect on the spectator; sometimes, even, a bodily movement which is all the more striking through not being accomplished in the normal way (for instance, a man using his foot to turn a door-key, the main theme of *Painting, 1978*). The search, often by the most roundabout means, for an immediately perceptible reality — or, more precisely, for a concrete resonance thanks to which the onlooker has the feeling of entering into immediate communication with the real — such seems to be Bacon's artistic endeavour, which is always conducted in a state of extreme tension, since it is through the active interplay of contrary forces — the urge towards realism and the desire to transcribe in total freedom — in other words, by more than a romantic, and purely external, juxtaposition of contrasts, that the artist has the best chance of achieving his aim: to secure the supreme manifestation of a presence in all its ''brutality of fact'' (the expression used by Bacon himself in his discussions with David Sylvester), and to subjugate the spectator by the peculiar life his gaze kindles in this presence.

But, for the two-dimensional figures inscribed on the canvas to be invested with such compelling life, although we know it to be artificial (independent of biology and a product of human ingeniousness), is it enough that the figure should appear not as a passive copy of a certain reality, but as an inventive, imaginative recreation of that reality, and should speak to us about something quite close to us in space and time? Whether or not Bacon has been aware of any inadequacy in this respect, the fact is that — no doubt spontaneously, and less through calculated effect than in the heat of the moment — he has never had the slightest hesitation in introducing irrational elements into the painting and organization of his pictures, and this influx of illogicality has given them a still greater charge of life. Not only has he always relied a great deal on what, in his conversations with David Sylvester, he calls ''accident'' (a drip of paint from the brush, whether fine or broad, a slip of the hand, or any other involuntary mishap modifying the intended effect) and has even gambled on a deliberate recourse to chance (by throwing paint directly at the canvas or rubbing it over with a rag, thus producing aleatory effects which have at least the advantage of reducing the ''illustrational'' nature of the given painting, and even of allowing work to go forward on a different basis), he has also often slipped in apparently gratuitous details without any thematic justification or, even if they can be accounted for by some artistic requirement, that requirement was sufficiently vague for the painter to satisfy it in a resolutely arbitrary fashion, so that the canvas, thus divorced from all ideal norms, patently bears the stamp of that contingency inherent in all manifestations of life on this planet. Such vagaries — closed or open circles, ellipses or indefinitely shaped blots, distributed, as far as one can tell, at random; pointing arrows, which not only catch the eye, but seem to be intended to deflect the gaze in a certain direction; or again, a long trail of white paint suggesting a sudden outflow or a whiplash — act as heightening accents in the sense that, having no meaning or being pure signals, they exist to some extent as capricious or disorderly elements (expressive of liberties taken or rules broken) in relation to the comparative order of the meaningful whole which, but for the touch of madness thus introduced, would be a more or less interesting or attractive or even fascinating composition, but not the thing, vibrant with life, that, in its essential uncertainty, it is.

Galvanize the figure or figures, punctuate the proffered spectacle according to whim, instead of obeying imperatives of composition (which would be to tend towards decoration) — such, in my view, is one of the golden rules applied instinctively, or so one imagines, by Bacon. This may explain why, for instance, he has sometimes taken a given figure and, by recasting or even twisting rather than by literally reconstructing it, squeezed it, wholly or partially, into a more restricted framework, supplementary to the general framework of the picture: this addition may be a totally non-representational, purely linear pattern which, at the same time as it serves as an intermediary term between the figure and the actual picture-frame, and up to a point helps to suggest the space in which the figure is supposed to be, seems to constitute a cage, visible only in bare outline, and into which the figure has been more or less packed, as though, in order to ensure maximum force, the freely and furiously painted part had to be enclosed, set like a jewel, or enshrined, just as, with the same purpose of intensification, Bacon sometimes puts it against a screen, another simple means of enhancement.

Whether he gives them definite location thanks to a semblance of geometrical patterning, or whether he supplies a background which serves to set them off, it seems that Bacon often arranges for certain parts of a picture to be isolated for emphasis, or to stand out as being the dominant parts: those which, because of their theme, are the most lively, and in relation to which the other parts are no more than a background, a place laid out for the action. It is with the same intention, no doubt, that he likes to lift his figures up, either by means of a modest pedestal supporting the piece of furniture on which the particular figure is seated or lying, or by frankly raising them from the floor (as in the 1970 triptych, which presents three female figures perched on a sort of long curved beam running across the three panels, or in another triptych of the same year in which the two lateral panels are occupied by a man sitting on a seat apparently attached to supports, like the seat of a swing). It is worth noting, incidentally, that Bacon, in discussing his art, reveals — as a simple fact, without trying to analyse its causes, which can be presumed to operate at some deep and decisive level — his particular interest in elevated figures, at least, be it added, when they are human. He mentions, for instance, that he was very impressed — from the secular point of view of the pure spectacle — by a photograph of Pope Pius XII borne aloft in the *sedia gestatoria* on the occasion of his enthronement, and he admits that what interests him in the theme of the Crucifixion is not the religious drama, with the divine victim as its central character, but — apart from the act of butchery objectively characterized by the event — the spatial position of the hanging Christ elevated on the cross. No doubt, Bacon's art, materialized in paintings far removed from any form of belief and, as he himself says, conveying no message, is much too secular and positivistic for the term ''sacred''* to be applied to it with any confidence. Nevertheless, it is the case that this same art, which he claims is no more than a game, and which brings him substantial rewards, a fact which he does not pretend to disregard but, on the contrary, humourously emphasizes (a debunking approach, resulting to some extent from Dadaist nihilism and from the calling into question not only of traditional aesthetic systems but of the very value of art itself, and therefore of the ''artistic'' attitude), does frequently give rise to works which can legitimately be regarded as having a sacred aura, not of course as a result of their content since — the point must again be stressed — they are profoundly realistic pictures, devoid of any transcendental allusion, so that what they offer is offered with no hint of anything beyond the given representation, but because each particular work seems to be ruled by conventions singling out certain elements which are made to appear all the more imbued with life through having been visibly separated off from the profane banality of the humdrum (saved from the commonplace, wrenched out of ordinariness, placed either literally or figuratively on a podium, by means of various devices underlying what painting has achieved in those areas where painterly frenzy has, as if by a happy chance, been unleashed). The isolation, by various methods of the figures as if, in spite of their prosaic nature, they were untouchable idols; their ambiguity, since, without being Expressionist, they are often distorted to the point of inspiring a feeling akin to that blend of ecstasy and anguish which is known as sacred horror, and which is perhaps experienced most acutely in those vertiginous moments, prompted by the most widely different causes, when we have the sensation of entering into intimate contact with ultimately revealed reality; in the case of several of the figures, a partial blurring which seems to give them a deliberately secret character, without in any way detracting from their realism; the solemnity of the overall arragement, especially in the triptychs, but innocent of any aspiration to the sublime, and all the more effective because of this; the frequent intervention, as in the paintings of previous centuries with their pious representations of donors, of assessors or sometimes of assessors once removed (assessors of assessors, as it were) who, like officiating priests or acolytes, seem to have their appointed place in some hierarchical ceremonial and to act as a guard of honour for the main figure, who is thereby invested with still greater prestige, just as, in other contexts, Bacon may achieve a heightening effect by painting pictures within the picture, such as male heads which are obviously portrait busts... Is it not legitimate to suppose that all these features are intended to confer one precise quality on the works in which they occur: the power to entangle the spectator in the toils of what might be called a *blank* liturgy which, having no transcendental references whatsoever, and existing only for its own sake, is all the more moving through being quite untinged by any dubious implications?

Being a realist, since, even when he allows himself to go beyond the bounds of verisimilitude, his ultimate aim seems to be to express life (the life we live and feel, the being in flux that each one of us is) and to produce work endowed with that presence which is its own peculiar life, directly perceived without any intervening haze of mental distance, — an authentic realist but an enemy of the anecdotal which, even when serious, never penetrates below the surface foam of reality — Bacon has taken care not to burden his canvases with anything strictly speaking dramatic, that is, not to bring into play any story-line which, being accessible to the intellect, might short-circuit, and thus weaken, the sensory impact of the work, and at most has made use of almost non-existent scenarios (the most pronounced, no doubt, is in the central panel of the 1965 *Crucifixion*, where a man, scarcely visible except for his tricolour cockade, is being molested by someone wearing a swastika armband, a detail which, according to the artist, has no historical significance and was motivated simply by the need to put a patch of colour in that particular spot and by the circumstance that the arm-band was suggested by an old coloured magazine photograph showing Hitler surrounded by other Nazis). The fact remains, however, that, being too devoted to life to reject even the mortal counterpart implied by its lack of fixity, he has on several occasions accepted the idea, not assuredly of drama — too close to everyday newspaper stories and too involved with narrative — but of tragedy which, while avoiding sentimental overtones, appeals to that part of his sensitivity affected by "the smell of death" he finds in places where butcher-meat is on display. Not only do the various *Crucifixions*, from which the Bible story was immediately and totally excluded, remain marked with a seal of blood (mangled flesh), but also a very early triptych (*Three Studies for Figures at the Base of a Crucifixion*, 1944) is based on one of the darkest themes of Greek mythology, the revenge of the Eumenides, and another more recent one (1981) was expressly inspired by the *Oresteia* of Aeschylus. However, it is obvious that even though this composition has a tragic quality, it is undoubtedly free of all pathos and devoid of the slightest theatrical element: the qualities operative in this direct and simple work are the firmness of the general structure and the marmoreal solidity of the figures presented, qualities in keeping with the true nature of tragedy which, unlike drama where the characters behave according to their feelings and the play of circumstance, makes its protagonists beings all of a piece, subject to harsh necessity or fatality. Here again, without any recourse to the anecdotal, Bacon displays his profoundly realistic approach even in the use of myth: what he puts on show for us is quite simply there, like an epiphany, and of too dense a texture for us to deny it. Such is also the case with the 1976 triptych, which preceded the one just mentioned, and has as its central theme a man

— a Promethean figure, one might say — whose head is being pierced and ripped apart by a bird of prey with out-stretched wings, a bird akin to the more modest one to be seen standing below the flayed carcass of an animal (apparently a pig) in the 1980 picture entitled *Carcase of Meat and Bird of Prey,* another work that it would be impossible to translate into a story or any sort of developed statement, but which achieves the tragic resonance of a sacrificial scene through the majestic quality of its structure and of the colour of the piece of hanging butcher's meat. Finally, it should be noted that, in painting the *Bullfights* of 1969 whose truthfulness is all the more astonishing in that they are not the work of an aficionado, Bacon dealt realistically with what many of us consider to be one of the surviving manifestations of ancient tragedy.

Behind their glass which, according to him, is a means of ''unifying'' material unevennesses in the painting, but which I suspect is also intended to temper to some extent the realistic virulence of the works, or perhaps to give a certain ceremonial dignity to the presentation of characters caught, it would seem, more often than not in the warm tangle of erotic exchange, or in the most commonplace waking or sleeping attitudes, not to mention the most grossly functional ones, or again to extend to the whole picture (including the flat background) and to finalize, thanks to an almost literal englobing, that process of setting apart, of removal from the neutrality of everyday life, which is achieved, as regards certain of its features, by the most diverse means, Bacon's canvases, at once so effervescent and so controlled, provide, for the spectator who looks at them as a whole and grasps them in their diversity, a striking image of this unique contemporary artist in all his complexity, a complexity I had hoped markedly to reduce by studying him in the mirror of his work. The hope was, more or less, vain: to portray Bacon's art, even with the help of his instructive discussions with his friend, David Sylvester, turns out in the end to be almost as difficult as to draw the portrait of the artist himself, and hardly more enlightening (more conducive to simplification). Failure would, then, be undeniable if, after this rapid survey which makes no claim to detect hidden symbolic meanings where none is meant to be looked for, it were not after all possible to suggest, in a very general way, the significance of Bacon's work.

Although the artist himself declares that he has no message to deliver, I have found from personal experience that his pictures help us, most powerfully, to feel the sheer fact of existence as it is sensed by a man without illusions. In this particular instance, the sensation is all the more acute in that painting — in a present time clearly established with a wealth of detail — appears abruptly as a presence, both for its own sake and as a source of images which, in works that are operative and immediate in the effect they make on us and in their temporal topicality, have as their only purpose to be an almost wounding presence. Moreover, is it not a fact that such art, almost every image of which represents a sovereign conjunction of beauty and its negation, echoes the dual nature of those moments that we appreciate as being the most specifically human ones, those in which — fascinated, entranced to the point of vertigo — we feel we are in touch with reality itself and are at last living our life, while at the same time realizing that our delight is flawed with a strange dissonance:

the anguish aroused by that hostile immanence, death, which any apparently total grasp of life reveals as being lodged in our most intimate being? It is perhaps this fundamental ambiguity, above all, which prompts Bacon, a hypersensitive artist with a fierce thirst for reality, to treat the reality he creates in his paintings as others might treat a sacred entity: using various devices, he puts it in inverted commas or singles it out for emphasis, as something marvellous, the ambiguous nature of which (half-magic, half-menace) incites us to stifle it as much as to laud it.

In relation to these canvases, whose deep-rooted modernity is not reducible to a mere surface piquancy, David Sylvester uses the word "relevance", thus crediting them with the quality of being exactly apposite, of doing and saying what needs to be done and said. These pictures, having no hidden depths and calling for no interpretation other than the apprehension of what is immediately visible, since the artist forestalls all ideological commentary by denying any intention of implying more than he paints, and being spaces filled with pure living presences indicative of nothing other than themselves, and therefore stamped with an absence of sense — with, in other words, *nonsense* — seem, in their dazzling nakedness of the very moment (a nakedness with neither hither side nor beyond and unencumbered by anything in the least literary), to be images in keeping with the inanity of our situation in the world as ephemeral beings, more capable than other living creatures of brilliant and pointless ecstasies. In short, they correspond to that modern state of mind, referred to in a previous generation as *le mal du siècle* — the ardent awareness of being a presence permeable to all the charms of a world not notable, however, for its kindness, and the icy certainty that we are no more than this, have no real power, and are what we are only for a ridiculously limited time.

Like Samuel Beckett, whose apparently non-mysterious sentences are reminiscent of the discreet emanations from a smouldering peat fire, Francis Bacon — without rhetorical inflation or mythological paraphrase and in ways capable of providing total enjoyment through the accuracy and vigour of the formulation, whereas by rights we should be overcome by the harsh truthfulness of what is being thus tacitly suggested — expresses the human condition as it truly and peculiarly is today (man dispossessed of any durable paradise when able to contemplate himself clear-sightedly), and consequently he can with justification be called a realist, however strong — on a less everyday level — the tragic element that comes through unmistakably in places, but is also explicitly expressed both in the *Oresteia* triptych and in the allusions to the Eumenides (direct in the *Three Studies for Figures at the Base of a Crucifixion*, and indirect in the free plastic paraphrase of *Sweeney Agonistes,* a poem in one epigraph of which, derived from the *Choephori*, Orestes speaks about his persecutors). While the most solid achievement of an artist of this kind, operating with a directly figurative intention, is to make the fascinated spectator immediately aware of the bizarre, indeed absurd, nature of his existence (as a contingent, but questioning, being with no transcendent dimension), at the same time he cannot do other — even without aiming at pathos — than show the appalling dark side of life, which is the reverse of its bright surface. As an authentic expression of Western man in our time, Francis Bacon's work conveys, in the admirably

Nietzschean formula he himself has coined to explain the sort of man and artist he is, an ''exhilarated despair'', and so — however resolutely it may avoid anything in the nature of sermonizing — it cannot but reflect the painful yet lyrical disturbance felt by all those who, living in these times of horror spangled with enchantment, can contemplate them with lucidity.

*Michel Leiris*

(Translated by John Weightman)

ILLUSTRATIONS

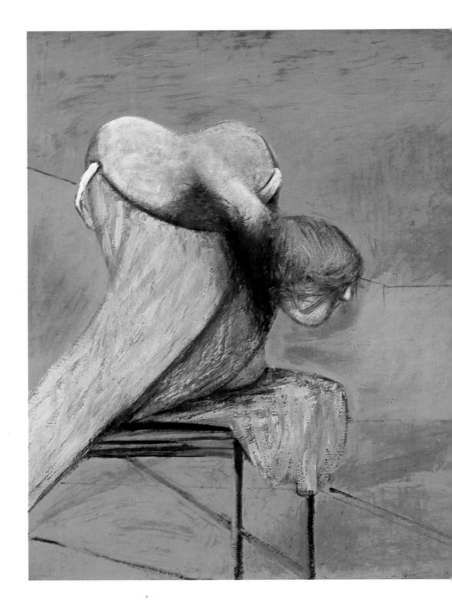

1
**Three Studies for Figures at
the Base of a Crucifixion.** 1944.
Oil and pastel on cardboard,
each panel 37 × 29 in./94 × 74 cm.
The Tate Gallery, London.

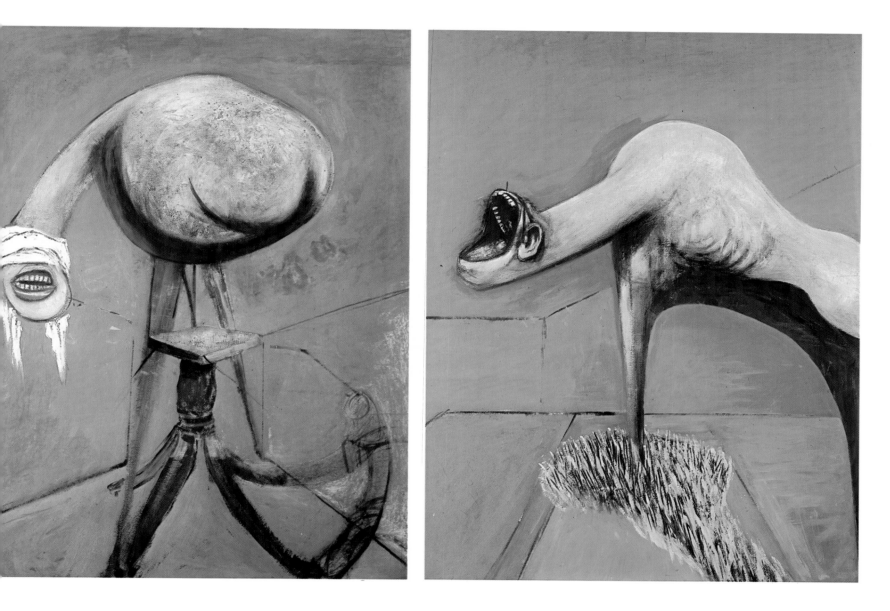

2
**Figure in a Landscape.** 1945.
Oil and pastel on canvas,
57 × 50$^{1}$/$_{2}$ in./145 × 128 cm.
The Tate Gallery, London.

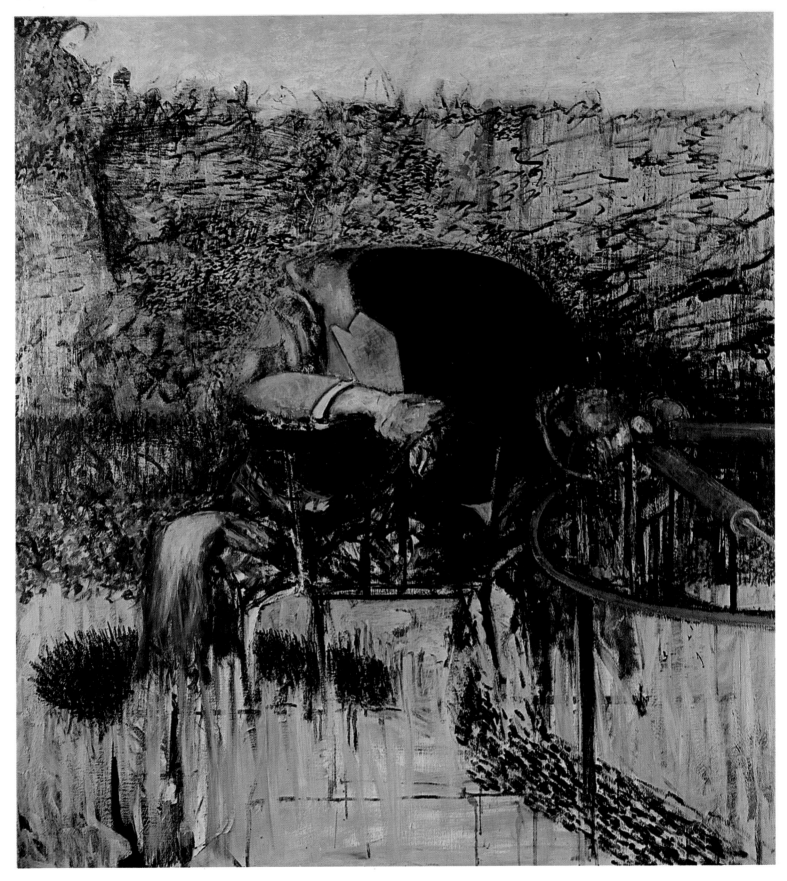

3
**Figure Study I.** 1945-46.
Oil on canvas,
48$^{1}/_{2}$ × 41$^{1}/_{2}$ in./123 × 105.5 cm.
Private collection, England.

**4**
**Painting.** 1946.
Oil and tempera on canvas,
78 × 52 in./198 × 132 cm.
The Museum of Modern Art,
New York.

**5**
**Head I.** 1948.
Oil and tempera on cardboard,
40¹/₂ × 29¹/₂ in./103 × 75 cm.
Collection Richard S. Zeisler,
New York.

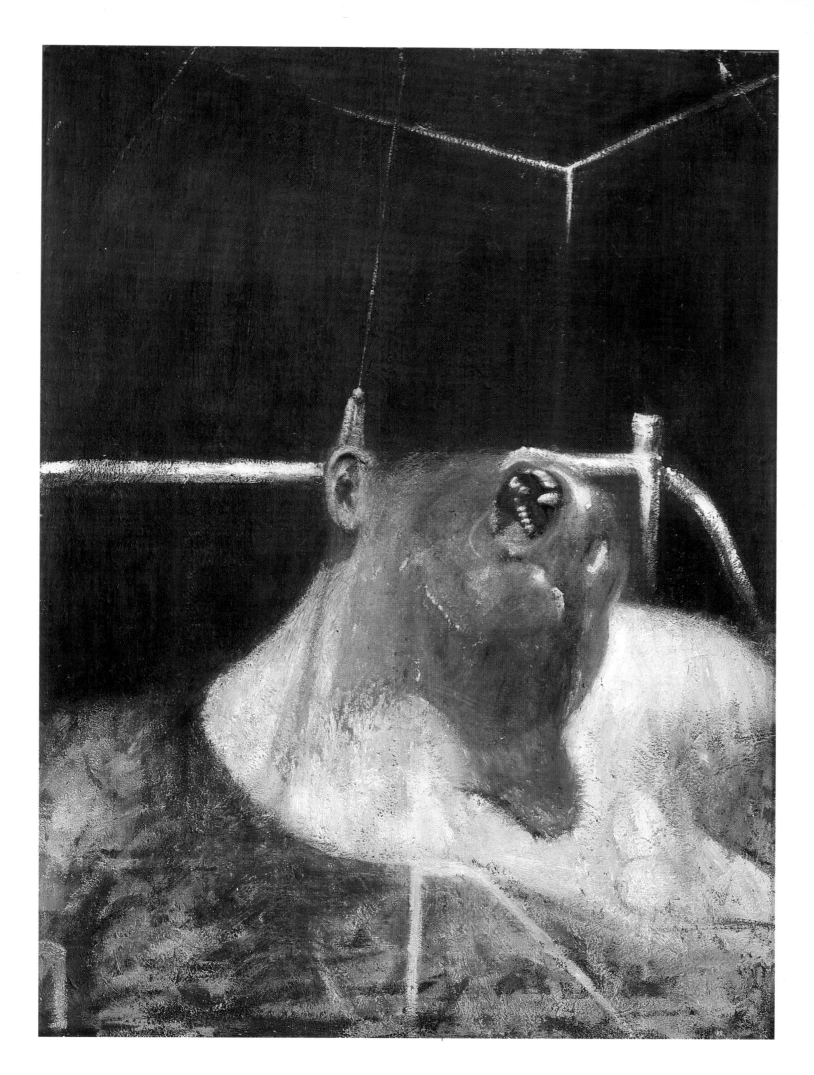

6
**Head VI.** 1949.
Oil on canvas,
36³/₄ × 30¹/₄ in./
93 × 77 cm.
The Arts Council of
Great Britain, London.

7
**Head III.** 1949.
Oil on canvas,
32 × 26 in./
81 × 66 cm.
Private collection,
Switzerland.

8
Study from the
Human Body. 1949.
Oil on canvas,
58 × 51 1/2 in./
147.5 × 131 cm.
The National
Gallery of Melbourne
(Felton Bequest).

9
Study for
Crouching Nude. 1952.
Oil on canvas,
78 × 53 7/8 in./198 × 137 cm.
The Detroit Institute of Arts
(Gift of Mr. William R.
Valentiner, Detroit).

**10**
Dog. 1952.
Oil on canvas,
78$^{1}/_{4}$ × 54$^{1}/_{4}$ in./199 × 138 cm.
The Museum of Modern Art, New York.

11
**Study after Velázquez's**
**Portrait of**
**Pope Innocent X.** 1953.
Oil on canvas,
60 1/4 × 46 1/2 in./153 × 118 cm.
Des Moines Art Center, Iowa.

**12**
**Man with Dog.** 1953.
Oil on canvas,
60 × 46 in./152.5 × 117 cm.
Albright-Knox Art Gallery,
Buffalo, N.Y.

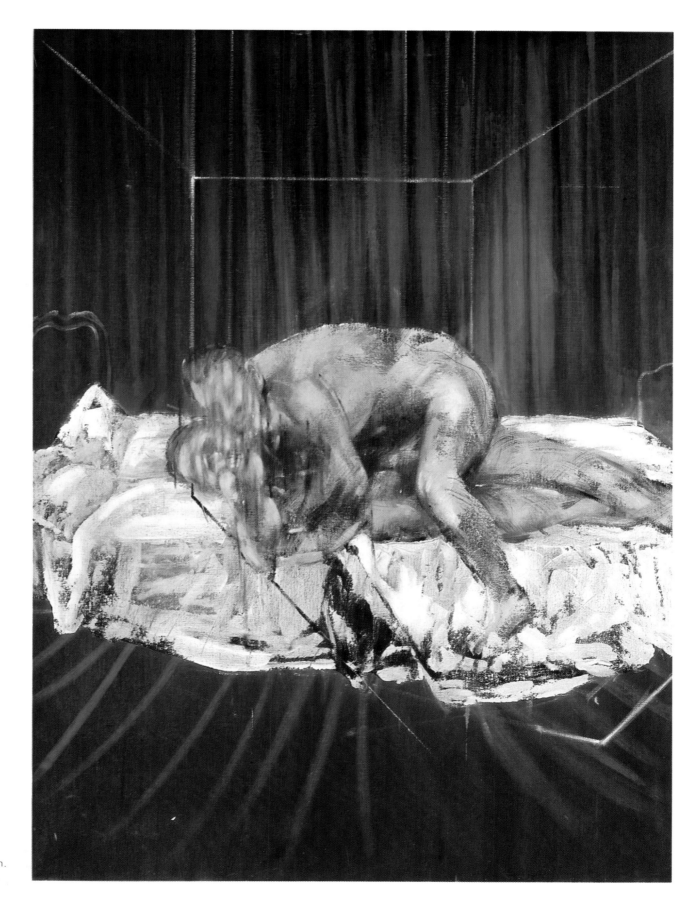

**13**
**Two Figures.** 1953.
Oil on canvas,
60 × 45⁷/₈ in./152.5 × 116.5 cm.
Private collection, England.

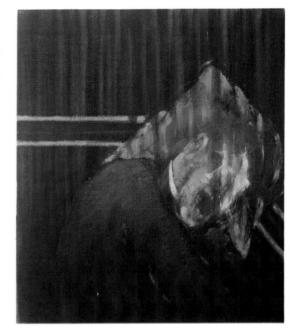

14
**Three Studies of the Human Head.** 1953.
Triptych.
Oil on canvas,
each panel 24 × 20 in./61 × 51 cm.
Private collection.

**15**
**Study for a Portrait.** 1953.
Oil on canvas,
60 × 46 ¹/₂ in./152 × 118 cm.
Kunsthalle, Hamburg.

**16**
**Chimpanzee.** 1955.
Oil on canvas,
60 × 46 in./152.5 × 117 cm.
Staatsgalerie, Stuttgart.

**17**
**Study for Figure IV.** 1956-57.
Oil on canvas,
60 × 46 in./152.5 × 117 cm.
National Gallery of
South Australia, Adelaide.

**18**
**Study for Portrait
of Van Gogh II.** 1957.
Oil on canvas,
78 × 56 in./198 × 142
Collection Edwin Janss,
Thousand Oaks, Californ

**19**
**Study for Portrait
of Van Gogh VI.** 1957
Oil on canvas,
79³/4 × 56 in./
202.5 × 142 cm.
The Arts Council
of Great Britain,
London.

**20**
**Three Studies for a Crucifixion.** 1962.
Triptych.
Oil on canvas,
each panel 78 × 57 in./198 × 145 cm.
The Solomon R. Guggenheim Museum, New York.

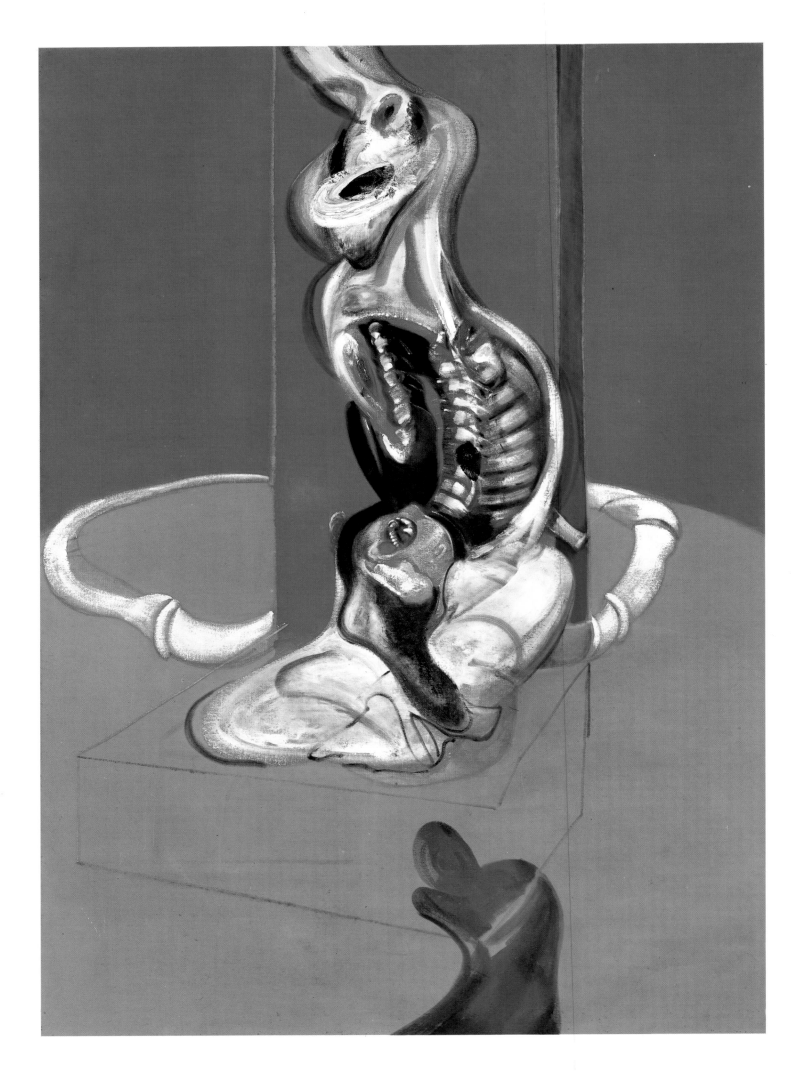

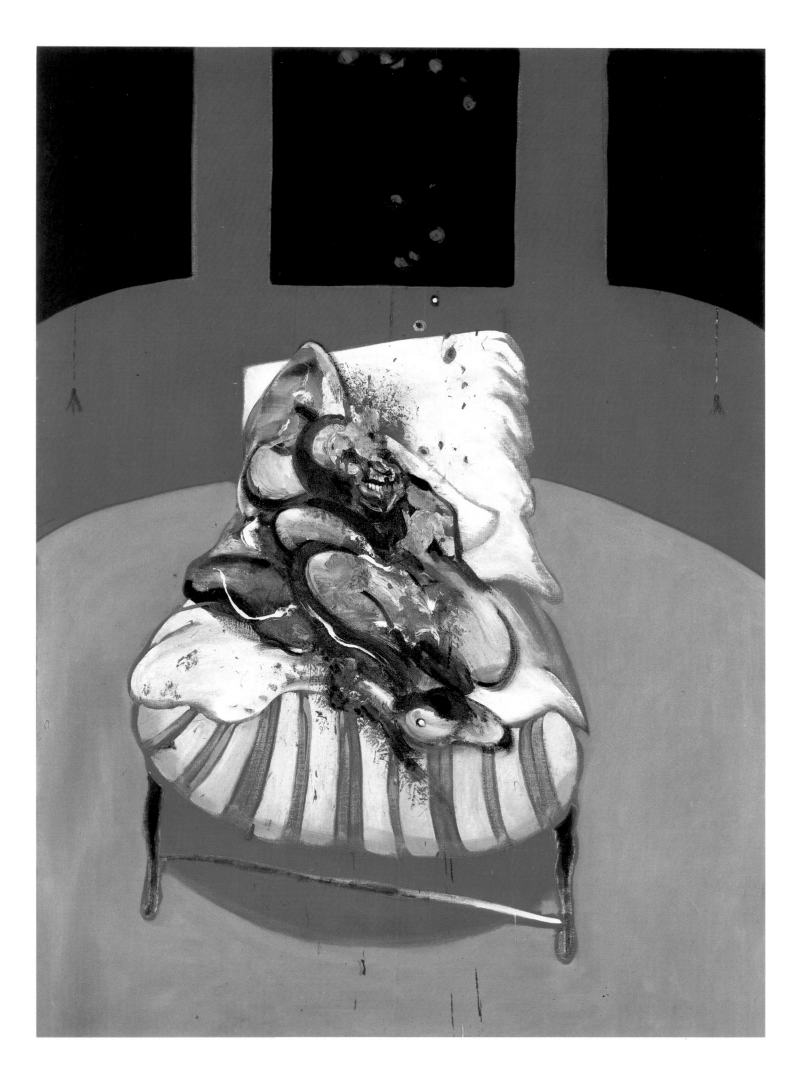

**21**
**Study from**
**Innocent X.** 1962.
Oil on canvas,
78 × 55³/4 in./
198 × 141.5 cm.
Collection M. Riklis,
New York.

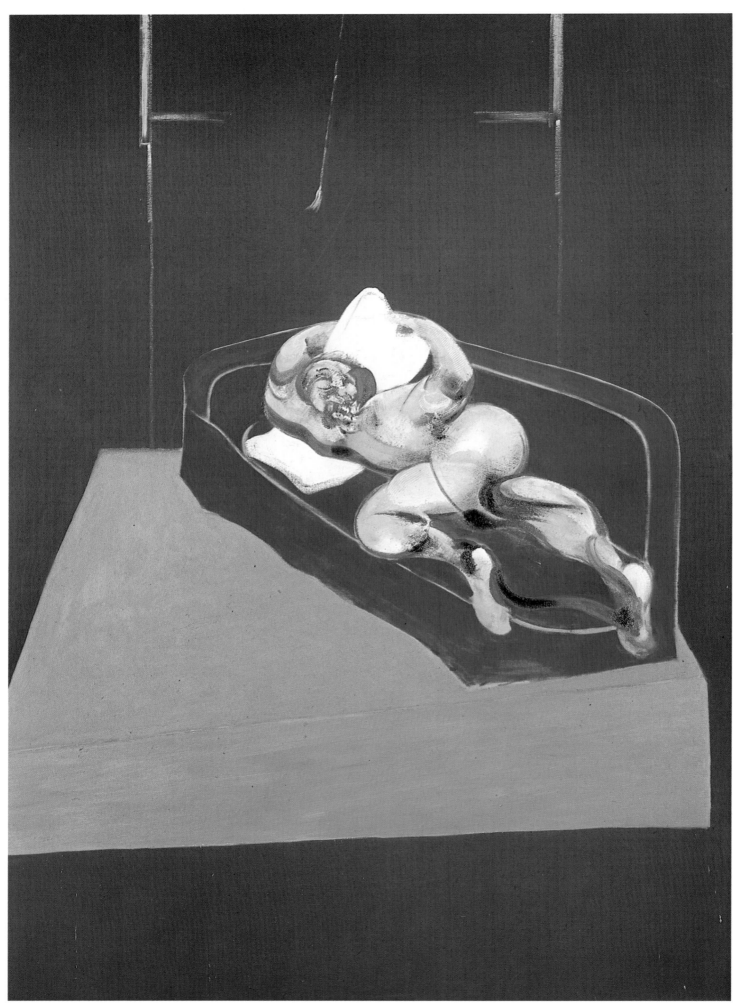

**22**
**Figure in a room.**
1962.
Oil on canvas,
78 × 57 in./
198 × 147 cm.
Galleria Galatea,
Milan.

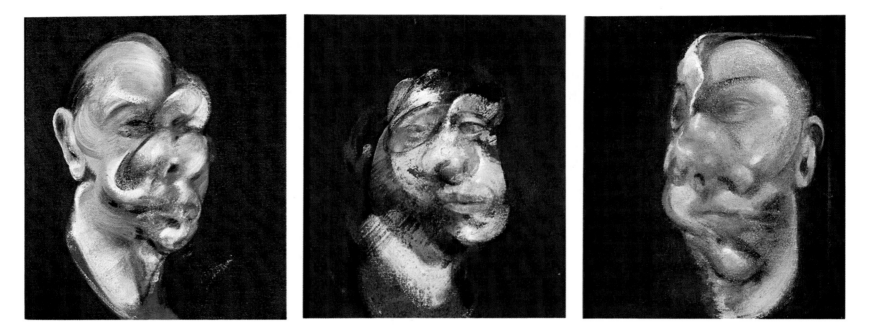

**23**
**Study for Three Heads.** 1962.
Small triptych.
Oil on canvas,
each panel 14 × 12 in./35.5 × 30.5 cm.
Collection William S. Paley, New York.

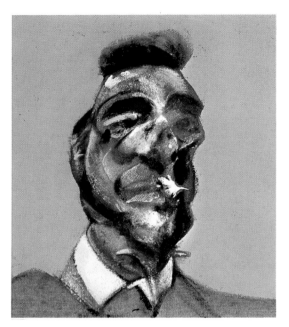 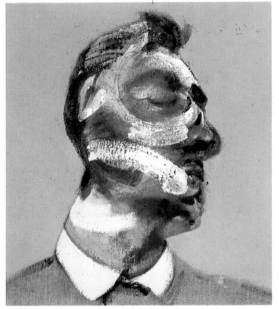 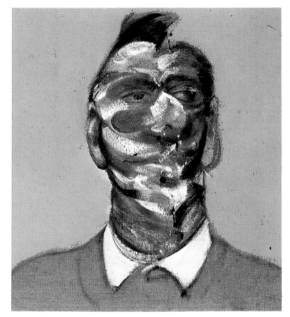

**24**
**Three Studies for Portrait of George**
**Dyer (on light ground).** 1964.
Small triptych.
Oil on canvas,
each panel 14 × 12 in./35.5 × 30.5 cm.
Private collection.

**25**
**Lying Figure with Hypodermic**
**Syringe.** 1963.
Oil on canvas,
78 × 57 in./198 × 145 cm.
Private collection, New York.

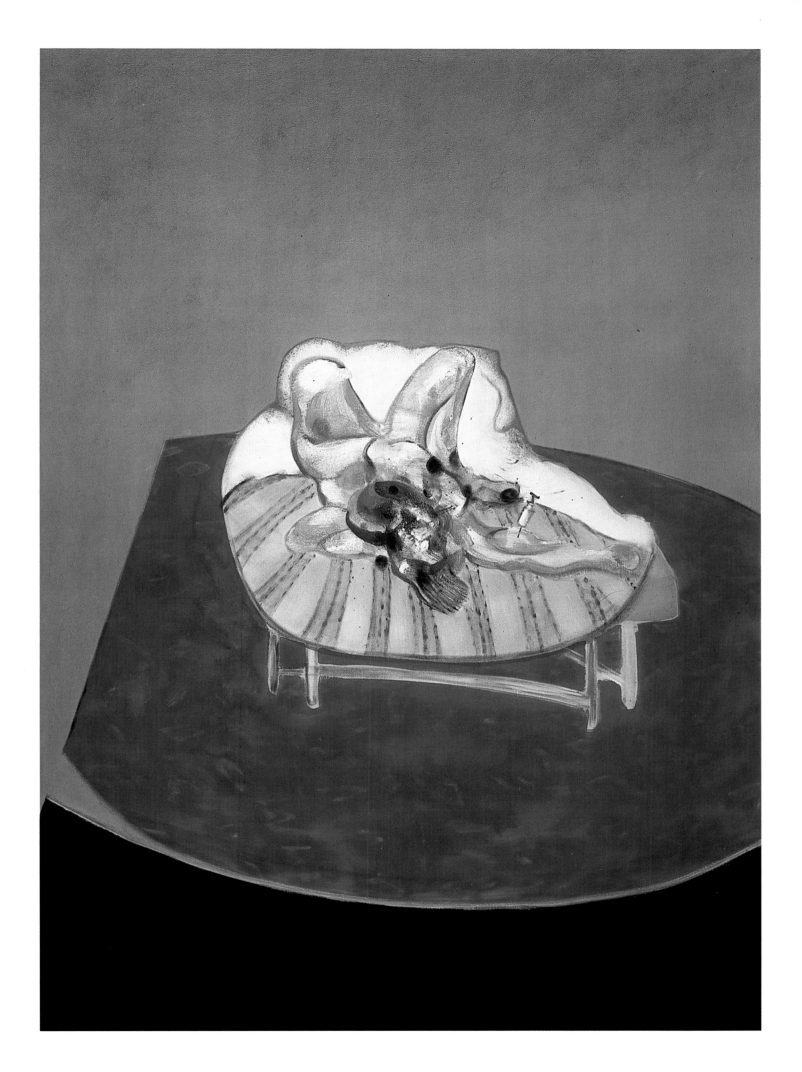

**26**
**Double Portrait of Lucian Freud**
**and Frank Auerbach.** 1964.
Diptych.
Oil on canvas,
each panel $65 \times 56^3/8$ in./$165 \times 145$ cm.
Moderna Museet, Stockholm.

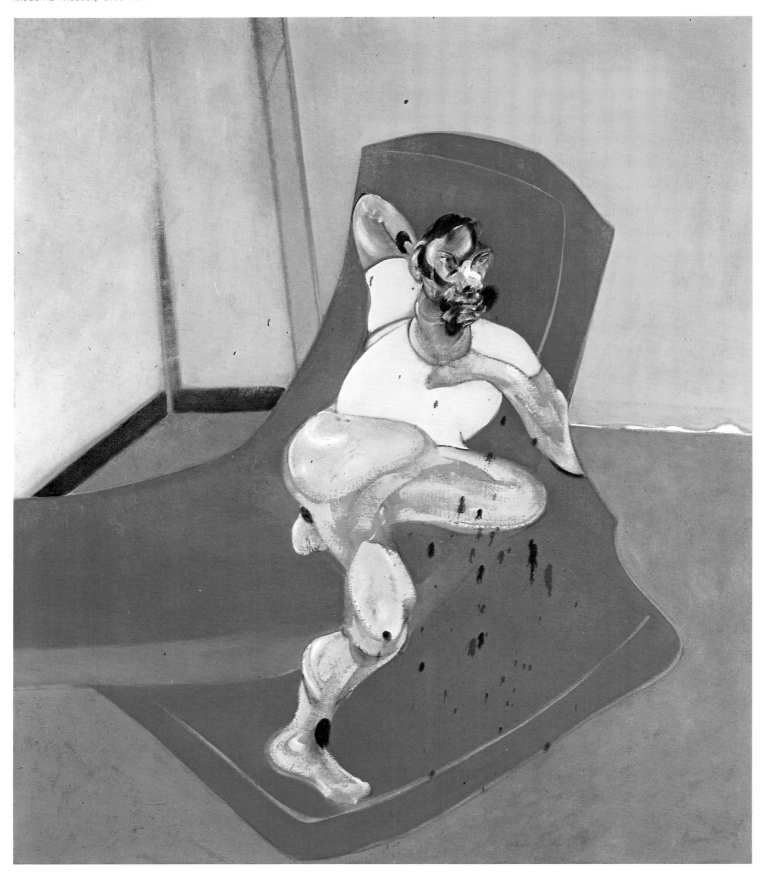

**27**
**Three Figures in a Room.** 1964.
Triptych.
Oil on canvas,
each panel 78 × 58 in./198 × 147.5 cm.
Musée National d'Art Moderne,
Centre Georges Pompidou, Paris.

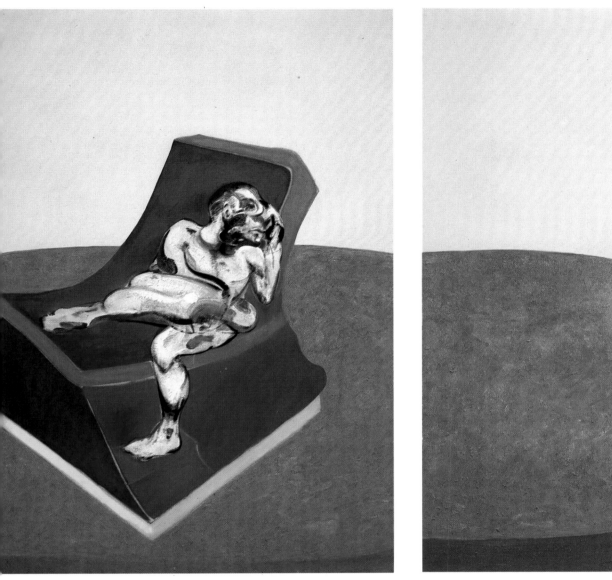

**28**
Crucifixion. 1965.
Triptych.
Oil on canvas,
each panel 78 × 58 in./198 × 147.5 cm.
Staatsgalerie Moderner Kunst, Munich.

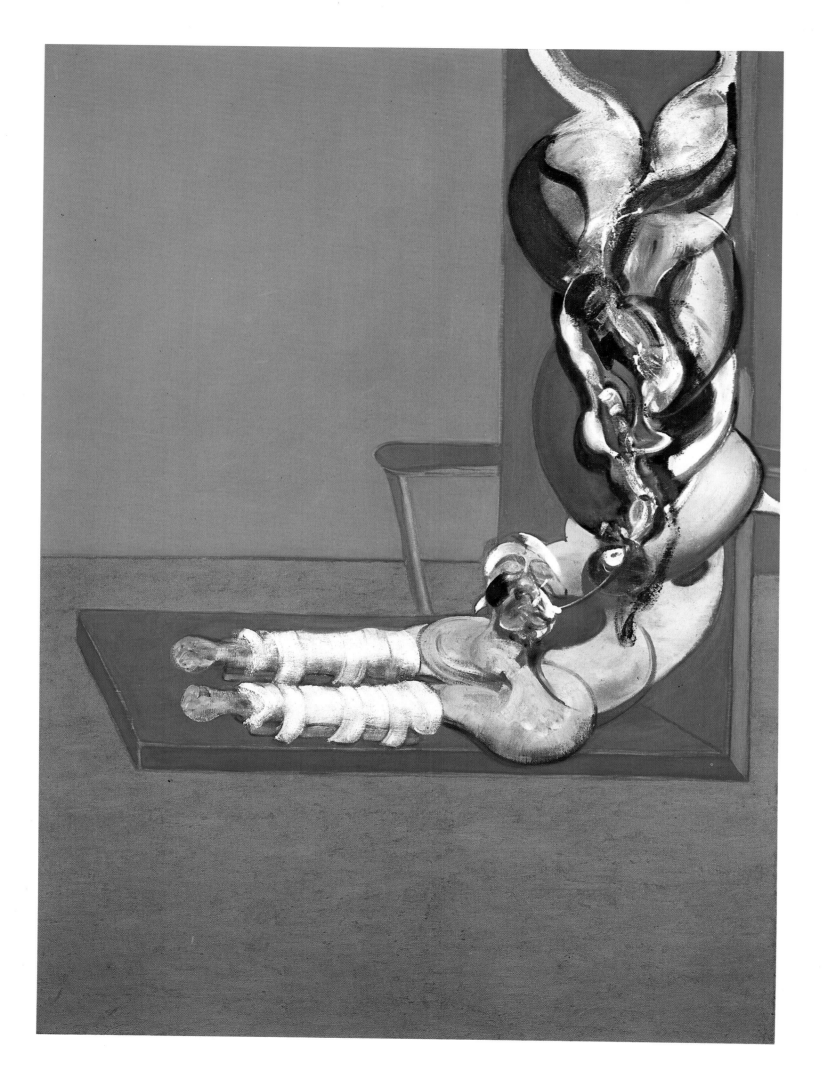

29
Study for Portrait
(Isabel Rawsthorne). 1964.
Oil on canvas,
78 × 58 in./198 × 147.5 cm.
Private collection, Milan.

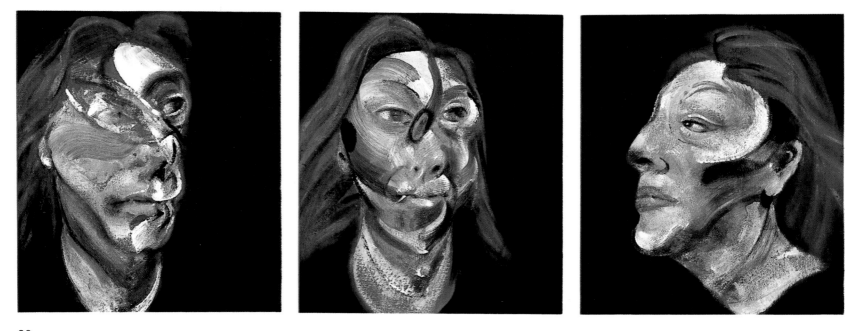

**30**
**Three Studies for Portrait**
**of Isabel Rawsthorne.** 1965.
Small triptych.
Oil on canvas,
each panel 14 × 12 in./35.5 × 30.5 cm.
University of East Anglia,
The Sainsbury Collection, Norwich.

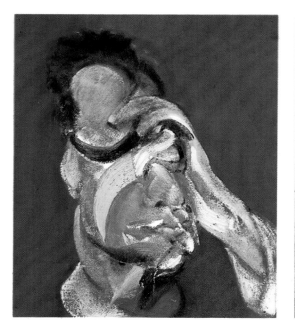 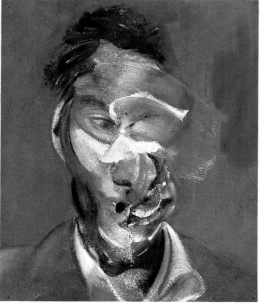 

**31**
**Three Studies for Portrait of Lucian Freud.** 1965.
Small triptych.
Oil on canvas,
each panel 14 × 12 in./35.5 × 30.5 cm.
Private collection, London.

**32**
**Portrait of Lucian Freud**
**(on orange couch).** 1965.
Oil on canvas,
61 1/2 × 54 3/4 in./156 × 139 cm.
Private collection, Switzerland.

**33**
**Three Studies of Isabel Rawsthorne**
**(on white ground).** 1965.
Small triptych.
Oil on canvas,
each panel 14 × 12 in./35.5 × 30.5 cm.
Private collection, Switzerland.

**34**
**From Muybridge — Studies of the Human**
**Body — Woman emptying a Bowl of Water,**
**and Paralytic Child on all Fours.** 1965.
Oil on canvas,
78 × 58 in./198 × 147.5 cm.
Stedelijk Museum, Amsterdam.

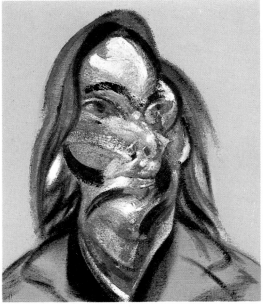

**35**
**Three Studies of Isabel Rawsthorne**
**(on light ground).** 1965.
Small triptych.
Oil on canvas,
each panel 14 × 12 in./35.5 × 30.5 cm.
Private collection.

**36**
**Three Studies of Isabel Rawsthorne.** 1966.
Small triptych.
Oil on canvas,
each panel 14 × 12 in./35.5 × 30.5 cm.
Private collection, Paris.

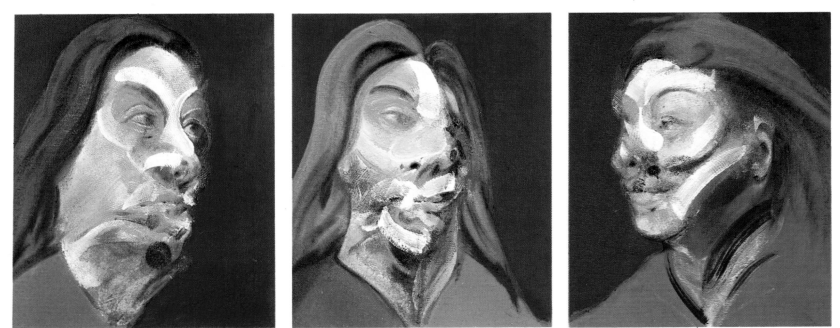

**37**
**Portrait of Isabel Rawsthorne.** 1966.
Oil on canvas,
$26^{3}/_{4} \times 18^{1}/_{8}$ in./$67 \times 46$ cm.
The Tate Gallery, London.

**38**
**Portrait of George Dyer Crouching.** 1966.
Oil on canvas,
78 × 58 in./198 × 147.5 cm.
Private collection, Caracas.

**39**
**Portrait of George Dyer**
**Staring at Blind Cord.** 1966.
Oil on canvas,
78 × 58 in./198 × 147.5 cm.
Collection Maestri, Parma.

**40**
**Three Studies for Portrait of Lucian Freud.** 1966.
Triptych.
Oil on canvas,
each panel 78 × 58 in./198 × 147.5 cm.
Marlborough International Fine Art.

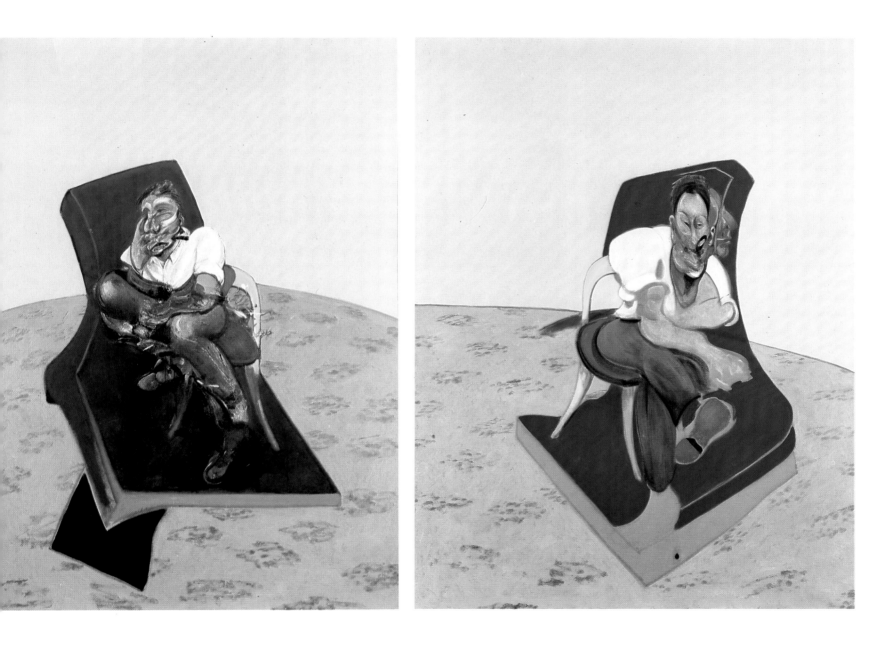

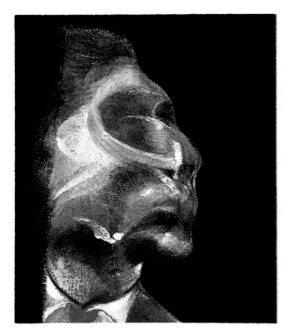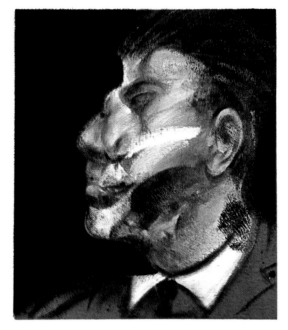

41
**Three Studies of George Dyer.** 1966.
Small triptych.
Oil on canvas,
each panel 14 × 12 in./35.5 × 30.5 cm
Private collection, New York.

42
**Portrait of George Dyer Riding
a Bicycle.** 1966.
Oil on canvas,
78 × 58 in./198 × 147.5 cm.
Collection Jerome L. Stern, New York.

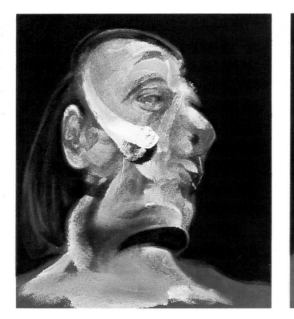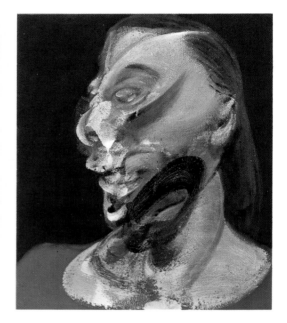

**43**
**Three Studies of Muriel Belcher.** 1966.
Small triptych.
Oil on canvas,
each panel 14 × 12 in./35.5 × 30.5 cm.
Collection James J. Shapiro, New York.

**45**
**Study of**
**Isabel Rawsthorne.**
1966.
Oil on canvas,
14 × 12 in./
35.5 × 30.5 cm.
Private collection,
Paris.

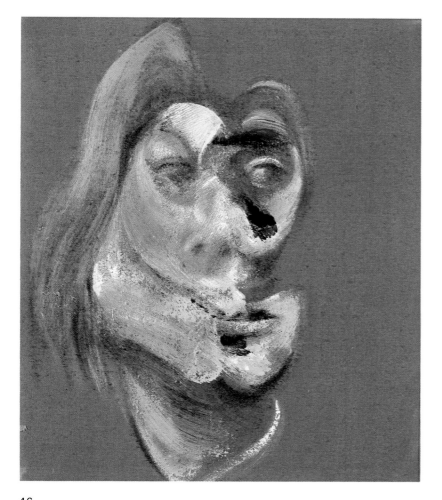

46
**Study for Head of George Dyer and
Isabel Rawsthorne.** 1967.
Diptych.
Oil on canvas,
each panel 14 × 12 in./35.5 × 30.5 cm.
Private collection, Italy.

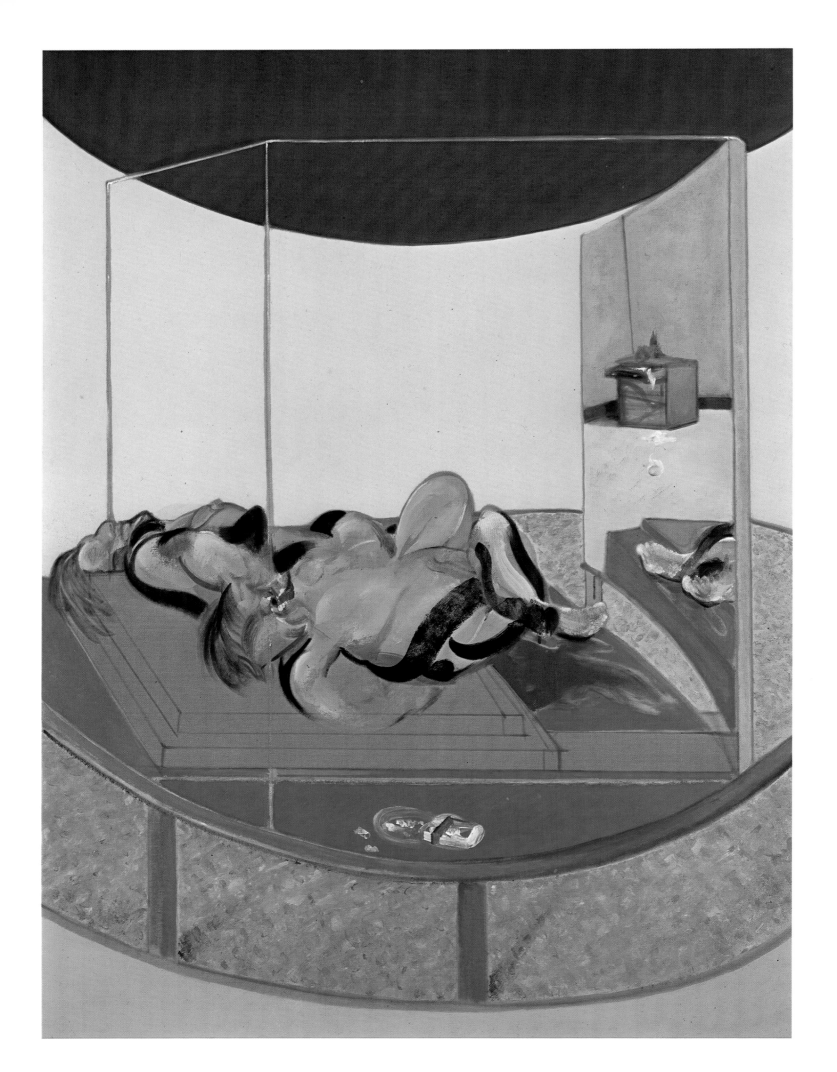

47
Triptych inspired by T.S. Eliot's Poem
"Sweeney Agonistes". 1967.
Oil and pastel on canvas,
each panel 78 × 58 in./198 × 147.5 cm.
Hirshhorn Museum & Sculpture Garden,
Smithsonian Institution, Washington, D.C.

**48**
**Study for Head of George Dyer.** 1967.
Oil on canvas,
14 × 12 in./35.5 × 30.5 cm.
Private collection.

49
Lying Figure.
1966.
Oil on canvas,
78 × 58 in./
198 × 147.5 cm.
Marlborough
International
Fine Art.

**50**
**Three Studies of Isabel Rawsthorne.** 1967.
Oil on canvas,
47 × 60 in./119 × 152.5 cm.
Nationalgalerie, Berlin.

rtrait of Isabel Rawsthorne Standing
a Street in Soho. 1967.
on canvas,
× 58 in./198 × 147.5 cm.
tionalgalerie, Berlin.

**52**
**Three Studies for Portrait.** 1968.
Small triptych.
Oil on canvas,
each panel 14 × 12 in./35.5 × 30.5 cm.
Private collection.

**53**
**Three Studies of Isabel Rawsthorne.** 1968.
Small triptych.
Oil on canvas,
each panel 14 × 12 in./35.5 × 30.5 cm.
Private collection, Nassau.

o Studies for
Portrait of
orge Dyer. 1968.
on canvas,
×58 in./
8×147.5 cm.
Museum Ateneum,
sinki, Collection
a Hildén.

55
**Two Studies of George Dye**
**with Dog.** 1968.
Oil on canvas,
78 × 58 in./198 × 147.5 cm
Private collection, Rome.

**56**
**Portrait of George Dyer**
**in a Mirror.** 1968.
Oil on canvas,
78 × 58 in./198 × 147.5 cm.
Collection H. Thyssen-Bornemisza,
Lugano.

**57**
**Two Figures Lying on a Bed with**
**Attendants.** 1968.
Triptych.
Oil and pastel on canvas,
each panel 78 × 58 in./198 × 147.5 cm.
Private collection, New York.

**44**
**Portrait of George Dyer**
**Talking.** 1966.
Oil on canvas,
78 × 58 in./198 × 147.5 cm.
Private collection, New York.

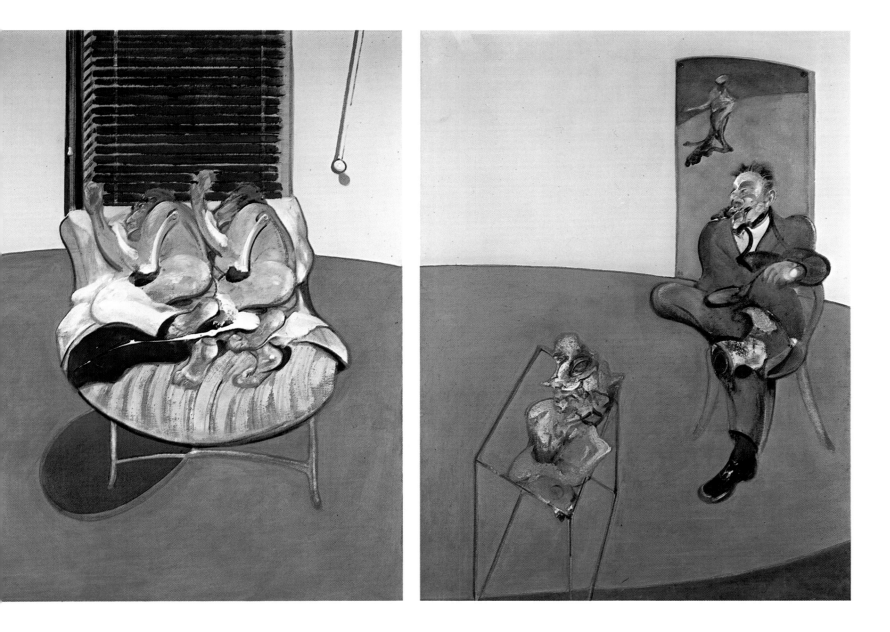

**58**
**Three Studies of Henrietta Moraes.** 1969.
Small triptych.
Oil on canvas,
each panel 14 × 12 in./35.5 × 30.5 cm.
Collection Gilbert de Botton, Switzerland.

**59**
**Study of Henrietta Moraes.** 1969.
Oil on canvas,
14 × 12 in./35.5 × 30.5 cm.
Private collection, Johannesburg.

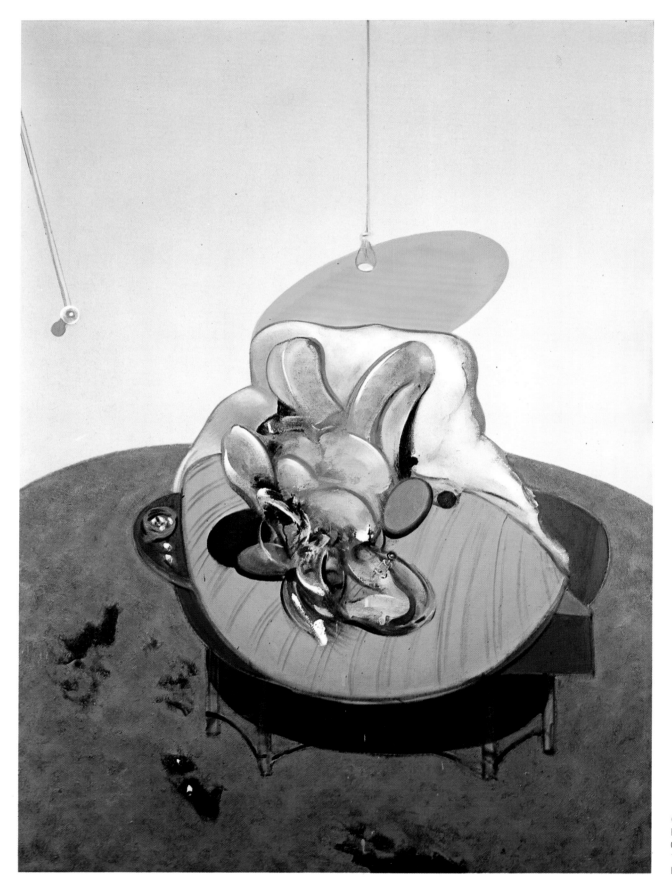

**60**
**Lying Figure.** 1969.
Oil on canvas,
78 × 58 in./198 × 147.5 cm.
Private collection, Montreal.

**61**
**Study for Bullfight No. 1.** 1969.
Oil on canvas,
78 × 58 in./198 × 147.5 cm.
Private collection, Switzerland.

**62**
**Three Studies of Lucian Freud.** 1969.
Triptych.
Oil on canvas,
each panel 78 × 58 in./198 × 147.5 cm.
Private collection, Rome.

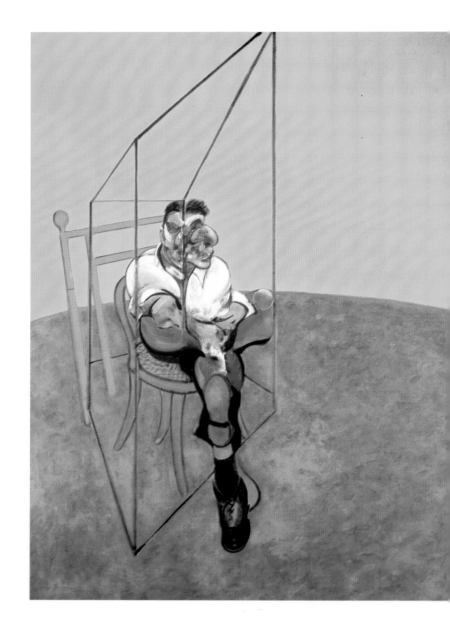

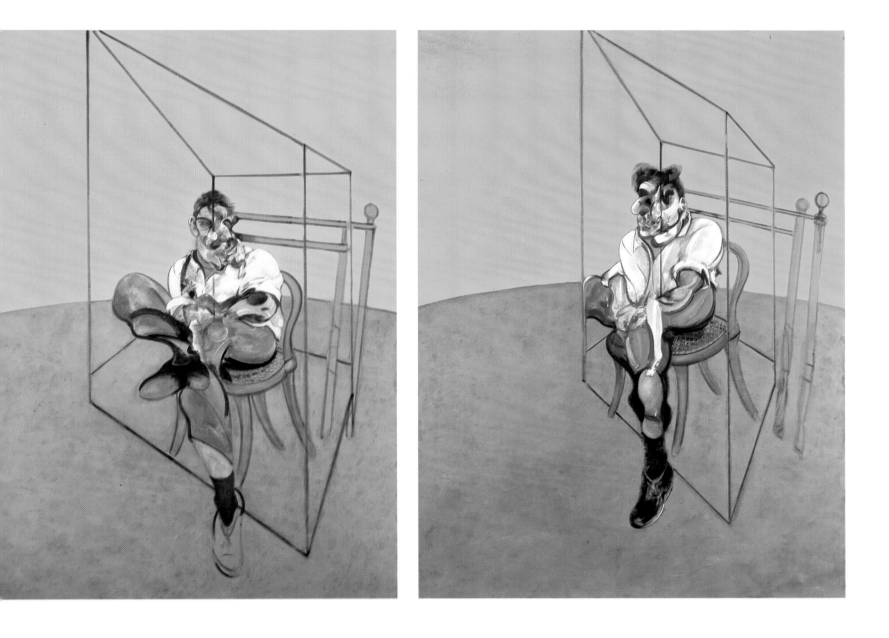

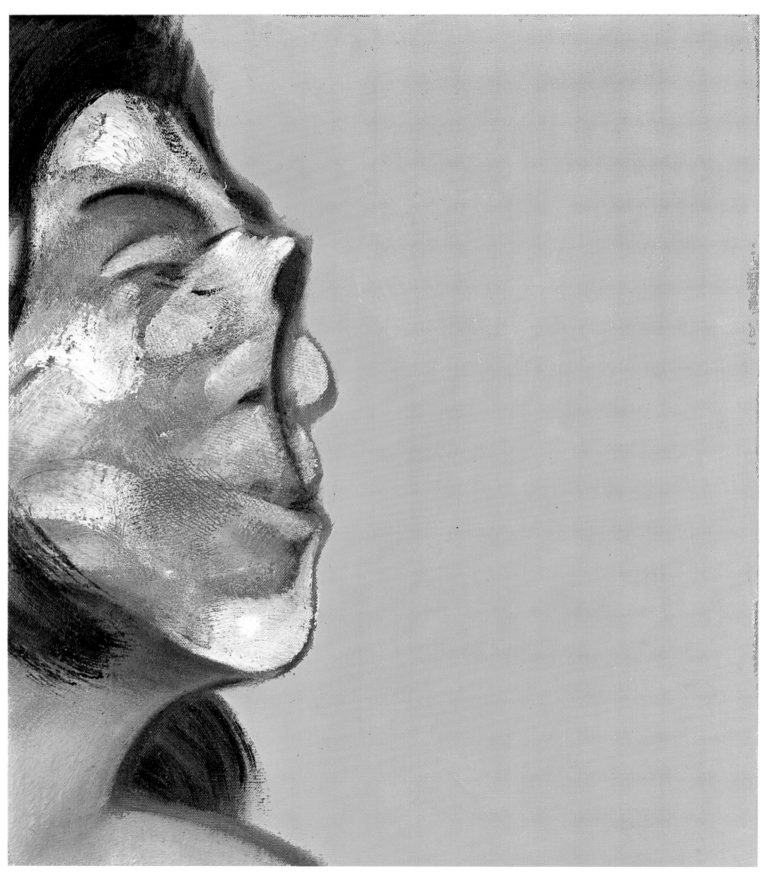

63
Henrietta Morae
1969.
Oil on canvas,
14 × 12 in./
35.5 × 30.5 cm
Private collection
Dublin.

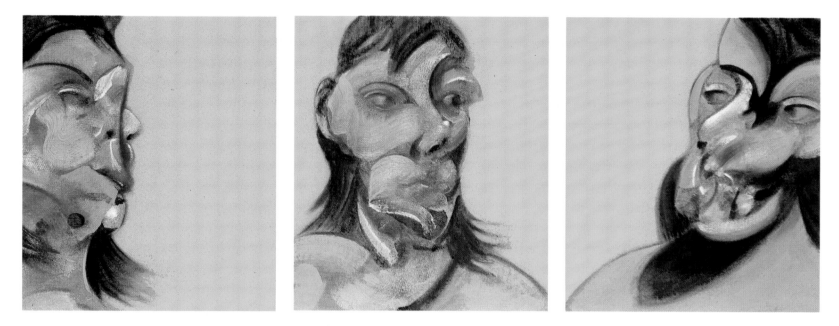

**64**
**Three Studies of Henrietta Moraes.** 1969.
Small triptych.
Oil on canvas,
each panel 14 × 12 in./35.5 × 30.5 cm.
Collection Galleria Galatea, Milan.

65
**Three Studies of George Dyer.** 1969.
Small triptych.
Oil on canvas,
each panel 14 × 12 in./35.5 × 30.5 cm.
Collection Madame Lucie Germain, Paris.

66
**Study of Nude with Figure in a Mirror.** 1969.
Oil on canvas,
78 × 58 in./198 × 147.5 cm.
Marlborough International Fine Art.

**67**
Studies of George Dyer and Isabel
Rawsthorne. 1969.
Diptych.
Oil on canvas,
each panel 14 × 12 in./35.5 × 30.5 cm.
Private collection, Switzerland.

**68**
Self-Portrait. 1969.
Oil on canvas,
14 × 12 in./35.5 × 30.5 cm.
Private collection, London.

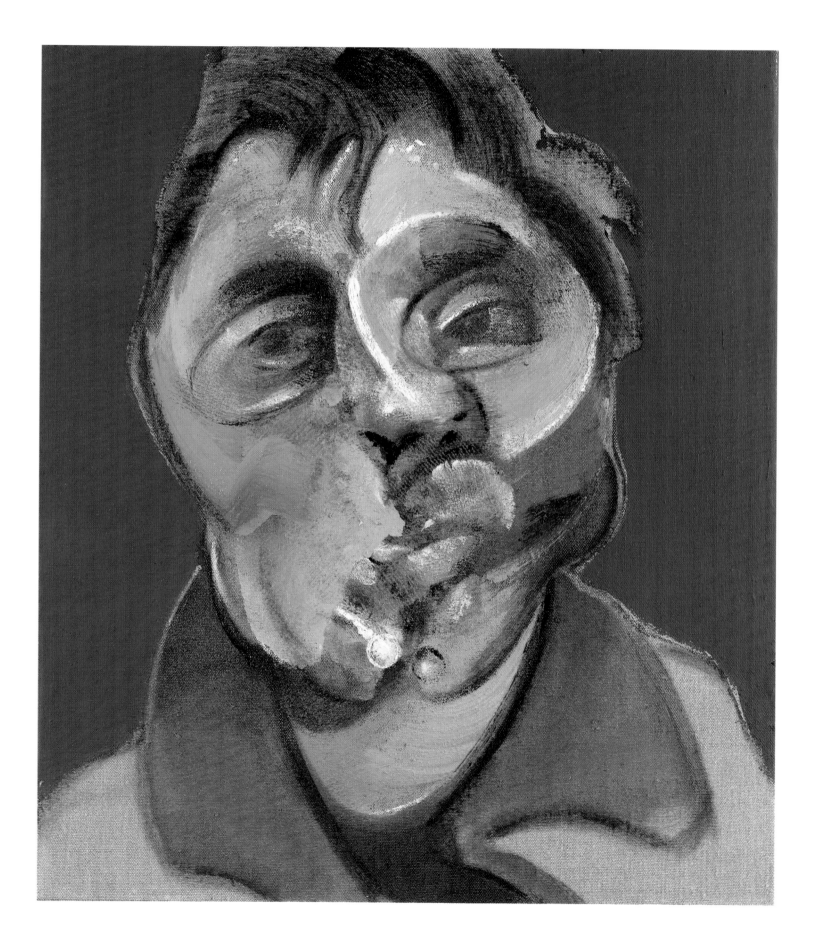

**69**
**Three Studies of the Male Back.** 1970.
Triptych.
Oil on canvas,
each panel 78 × 58 in./198 × 147.5 cm.
Kunsthaus, Zürich.

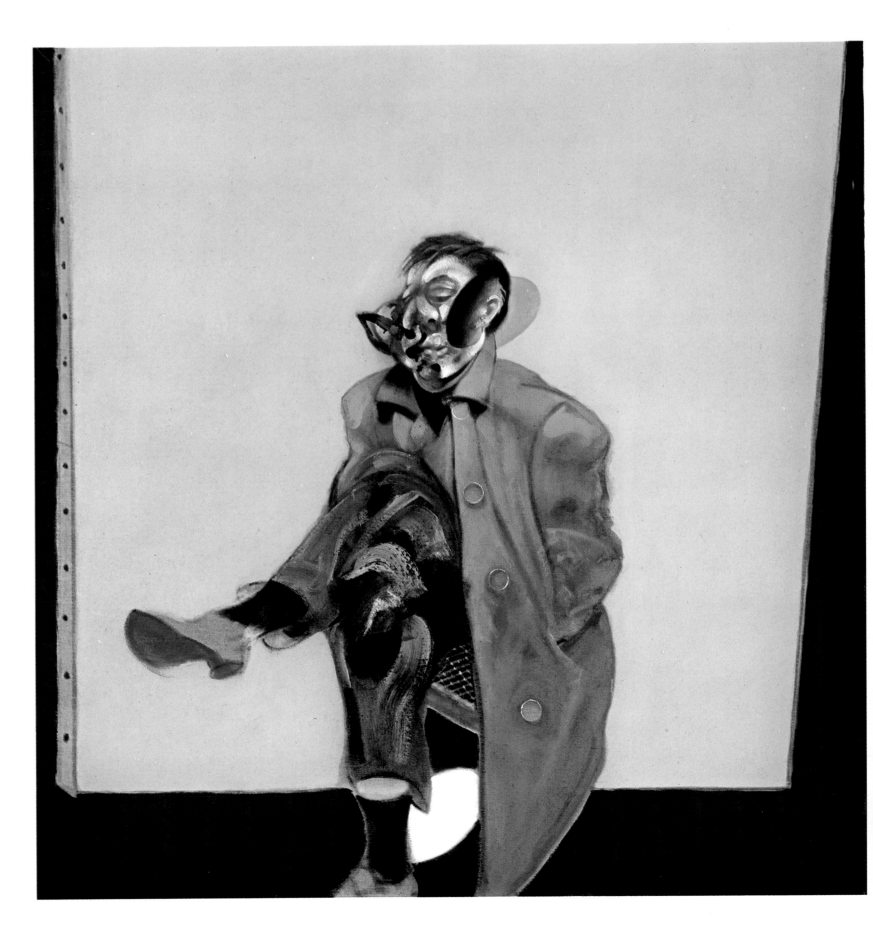

**70**
**Self-Portrait.** 1970.
Oil on canvas,
59⁷/₈ × 58 in./152 × 147.5 cm.
Private collection, London.

**71**
**Study for Portrait.** 1970.
Oil on canvas,
78 × 58 in./198 × 147.5 cm.
Private collection, France.

**72**
**Studies of the Human Body.** 1970.
Triptych.
Oil on canvas,
each panel 78 × 58 in./198 × 147.5 cm.
Marlborough International Fine Art.

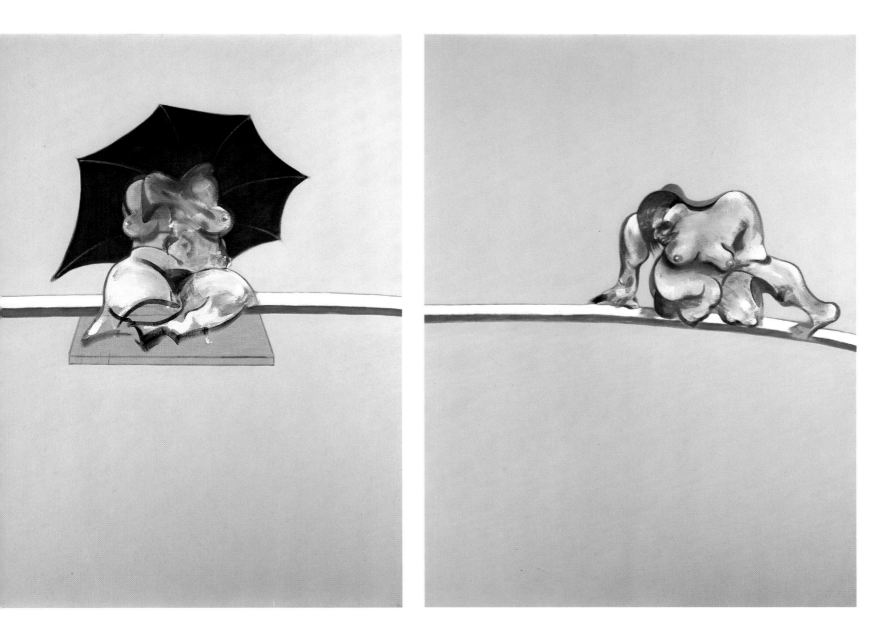

**73**
**Study for Portrait.** 1971.
Oil on canvas,
78 × 58 in./198 × 147.5 cm.
Private collection, London.

**74**
Second version of
''Painting 1946''. 1971.
Oil on canvas,
78 × 58 in./198 × 147.5 cm.
Wallraf-Richartz-Museum,
Ludwig Collection, Cologne.

75
**Studies from the Human Body.** 1970.
Triptych.
Oil on canvas,
each panel 78 × 58 in./198 × 147.5 cm.
Private collection, Switzerland.

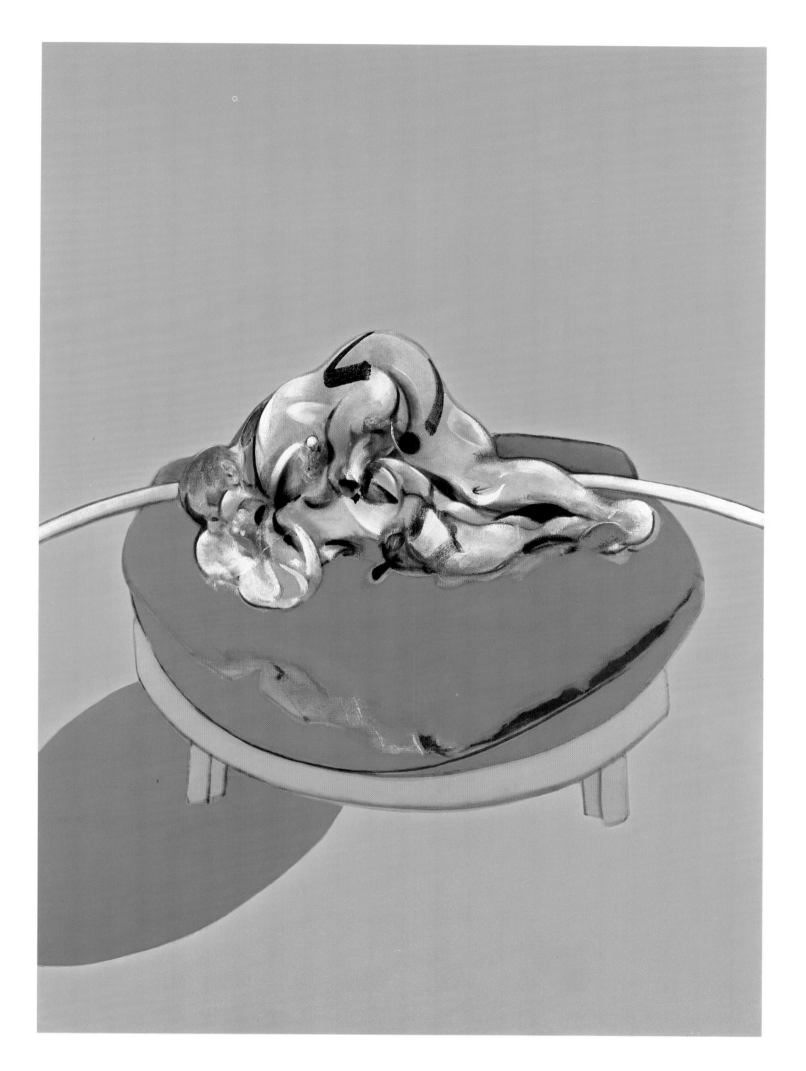

76
**Study for Portrait of Lucian Freud
(Sideways)**. 1971.
Oil on canvas,
78 × 58 in./198 × 147.5 cm.
Private collection, Brussels.

**77**
**Female Nude Standing
in a Doorway.** 1972.
Oil on canvas,
78 × 58 in./198 × 147.5 cm.
Private collection, France.

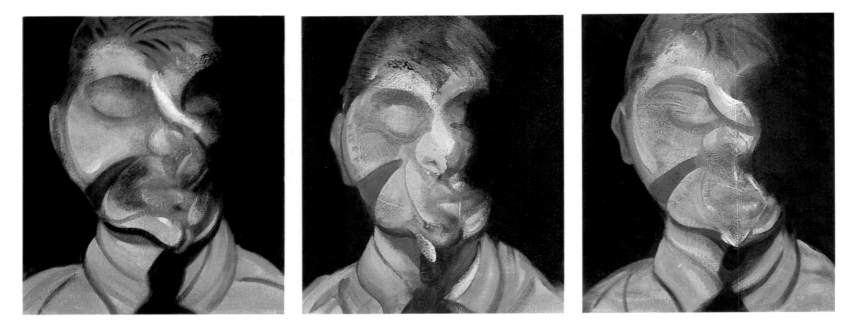

78
**Three Studies for Self-Portrait.** 1972.
Small triptych.
Oil on canvas,
each panel 14 × 12 in./35.5 × 30.5 cm.
Collection Basil P. Goulandris, Lausanne.

79
**Self-Portrait.** 1971.
Oil on canvas,
14 × 12 in./35.5 × 30.5 cm.
Collection Michel Leiris, Paris.

80
**Self-Portrait.** 1972.
Oil on canvas,
14 × 12 in./
35.5 × 30.5 cm.
Private collection,
London.

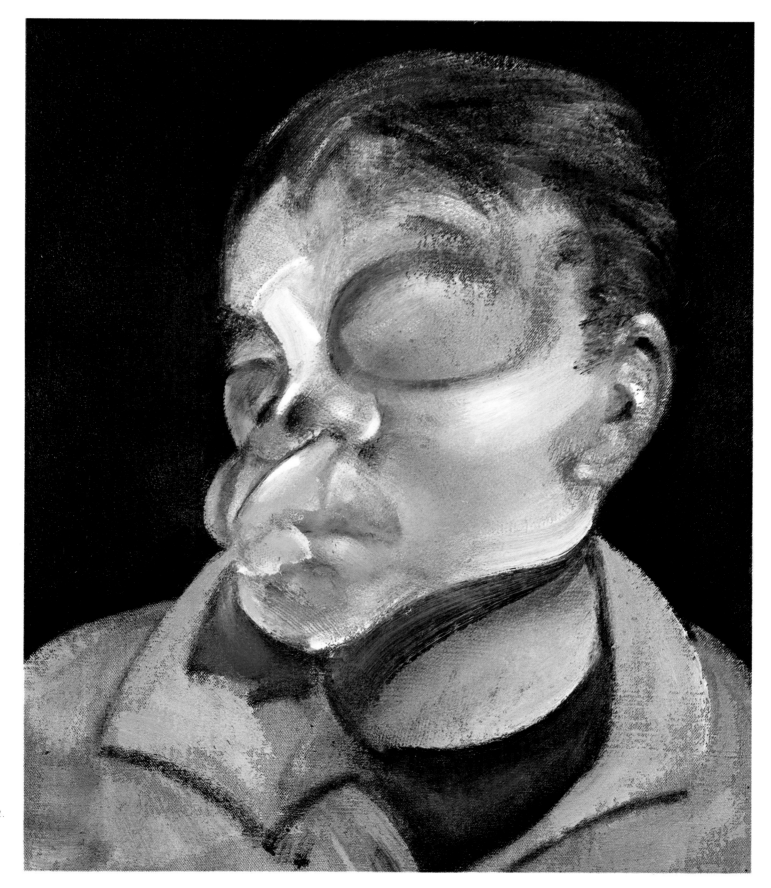

**81**
**Self-Portrait with
Injured Eye.** 1972.
Oil on canvas,
14 × 12 in./
35.5 × 30.5 cm.
Private collection.

**82**
Triptych. 1971.
Oil on canvas,
each panel 78 × 58 in./198 × 147.5 cm.
Private collection, New York.

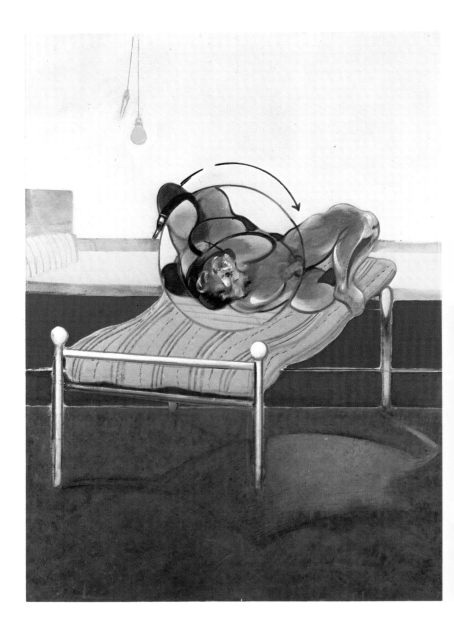

**83**
**Three Studies of Figures on Beds.** 1972.
Triptych.
Oil and pastel on canvas,
each panel 78 × 58 in./198 × 147.5 cm.
Private collection.

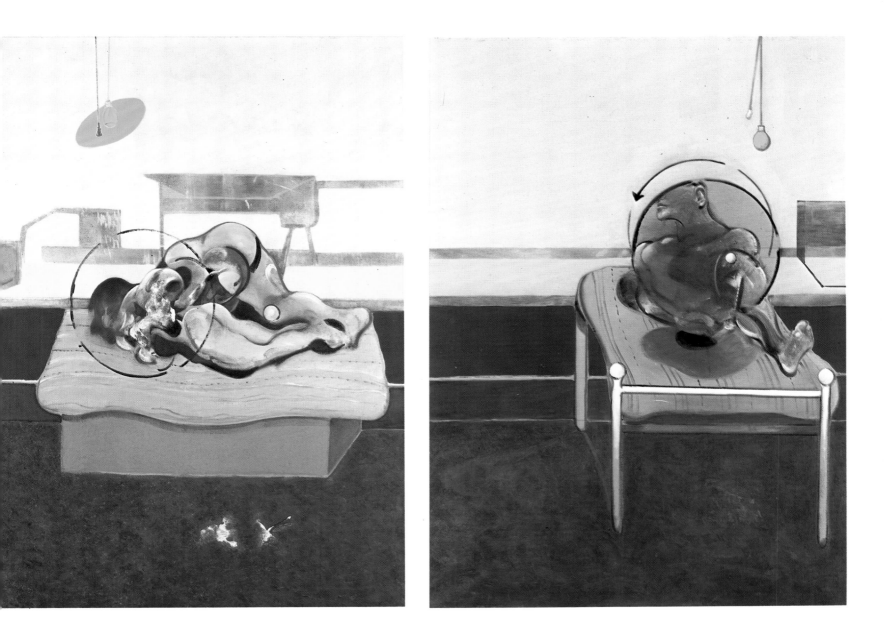

**84**
**Self-Portrait.** 1972.
Oil on canvas,
78 × 58 in./198 × 147.5 cm.
Private collection, New York.

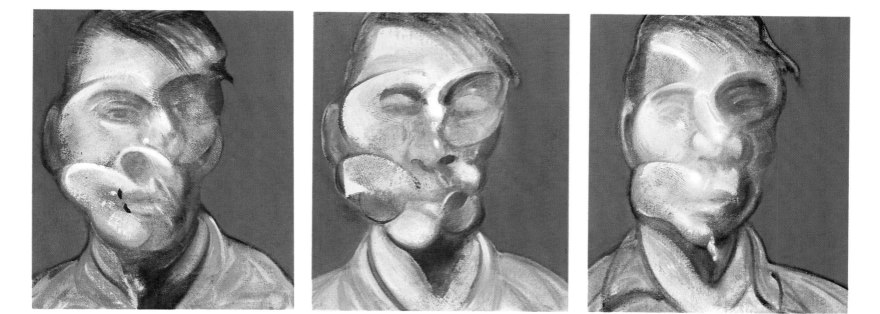

85
**Three Studies for Self-Portrait.** 1973.
Small triptych.
Oil on canvas,
each panel 14 × 12 in./35.5 × 30.5 cm.
Private collection, Switzerland.

86
**Self-Portrait.** 1972.
Oil on canvas,
14 × 12 in./35.5 × 30.5 cm.
Collection Gilbert de Botton, Switzerland.

87
**Self-Portrait.** 1973.
Oil on canvas,
78 × 58 in./198 × 147.5 cm.
Private collection.

8
Study for a Human Body - Man Turning
on the Light. 1973-74.
Oil on canvas,
78 × 58 in./198 × 147.5 cm.
The Royal College of Art, London.

**89**
Triptych. August. 1972.
Oil on canvas,
each panel 78 × 58 in./198 × 147.5 cm.
The Tate Gallery, London.

**90**
**Triptych. May-June.** 1973.
Oil on canvas,
each panel 78 × 58 in./198 × 147.5 cm.
Private collection, New York.

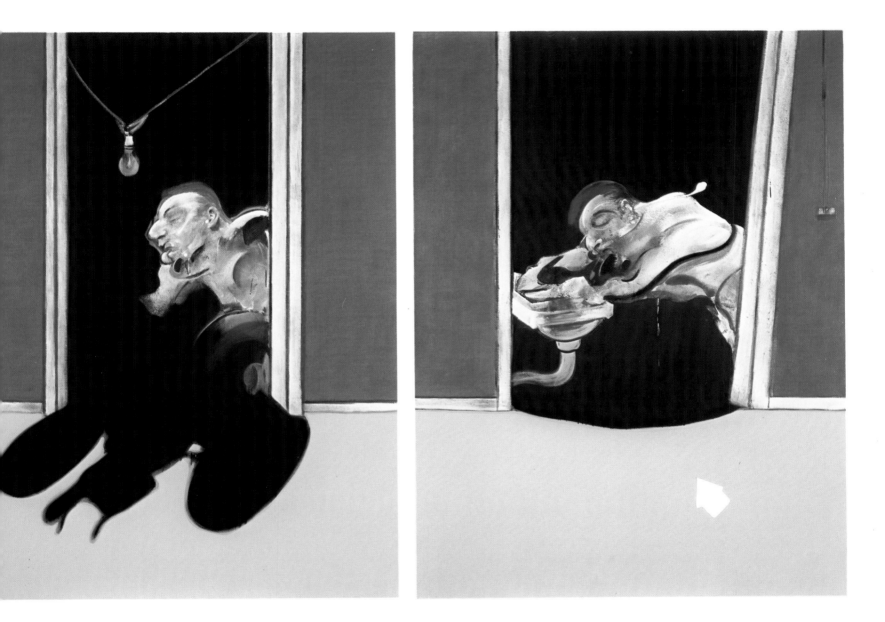

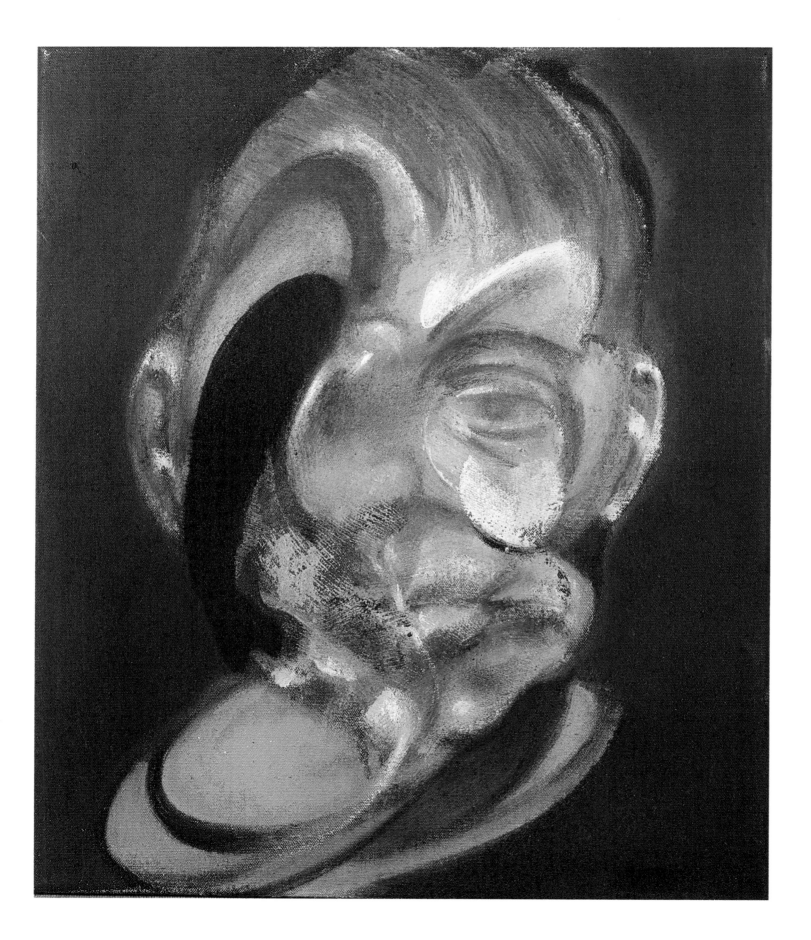

**91**
**Self-Portrait.** 1973.
Oil on canvas,
14 × 12 in./35.5 × 30.5 cm.
Private collection.

**92**
**Self-Portrait.** 1973.
Oil on canvas,
78 × 58 in./198 × 147.5 cm.
Collection Claude Bernard, Paris.

**93**
**Sleeping Figure.** 1974.
Oil on canvas,
78 × 58 in./198 × 147.5 cm.
Collection David Sylvester, London.

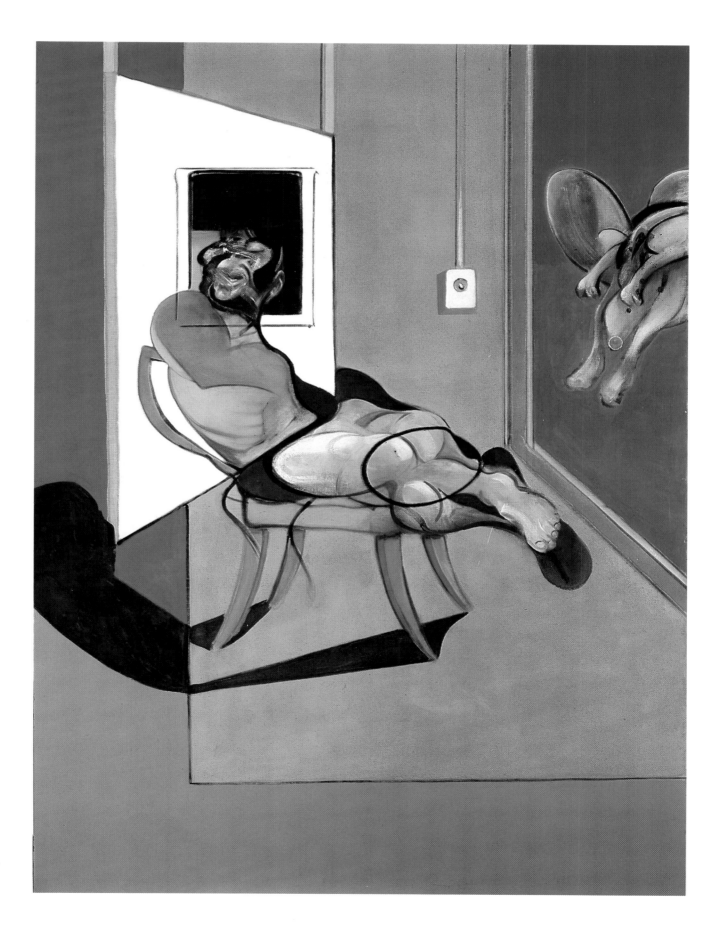

**94**
**Seated Figure.** 1974.
Oil and pastel on canvas,
78 × 58 in./198 × 147.5 cm.
Collection Gilbert de Botton,
Switzerland.

95
Three Portraits. Posthumous Portrait of George Dyer,
Self-Portrait, Portrait of Lucian Freud. 1973.
Triptych.
Oil on canvas,
each panel 78 × 58 in./198 × 147.5 cm.
Marlborough International Fine Art.

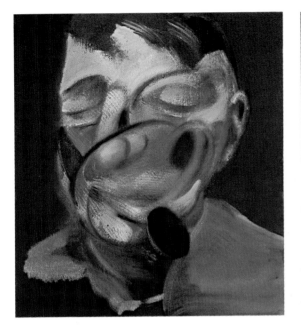

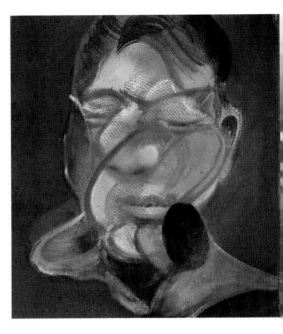

**96**
**Three Studies for Self-Portrait.** 1974.
Small triptych.
Oil on canvas,
each panel 14 × 12 in./35.5 × 30.5 cm.
Collection Carlos Haime, Bogotá.

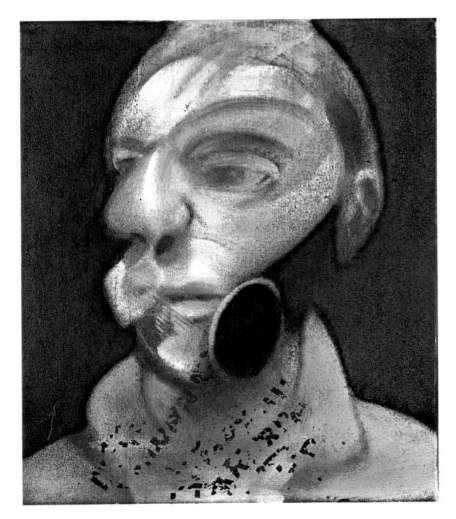

**97**
**Self-Portrait.** 1975.
Oil on canvas,
14 × 12 in./35.5 × 30.5 cm.
Private collection.

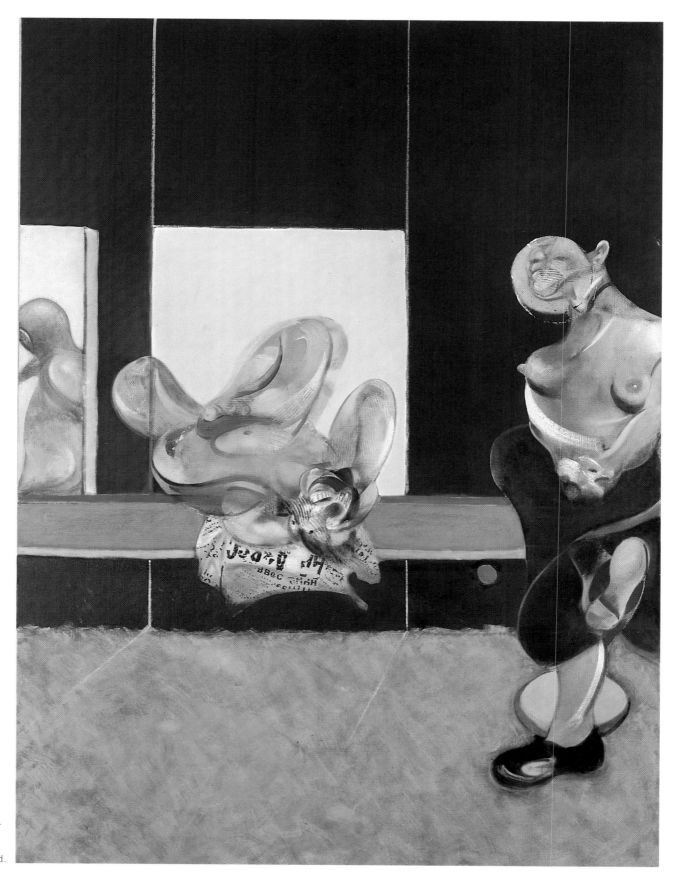

02
Studies from the Human Body. 1975.
Oil on canvas,
78 × 58 in./198 × 147.5 cm.
Collection Gilbert de Botton, Switzerland.

103
**Triptych. March.** 1974.
Oil on canvas,
each panel 78 × 58 in./198 × 147.5 cm.
Private collection, Madrid.

103
**Triptych. March.** 1974.
Oil on canvas,
each panel 78 × 58 in./198 × 147.5 cm.
Private collection, Madrid.

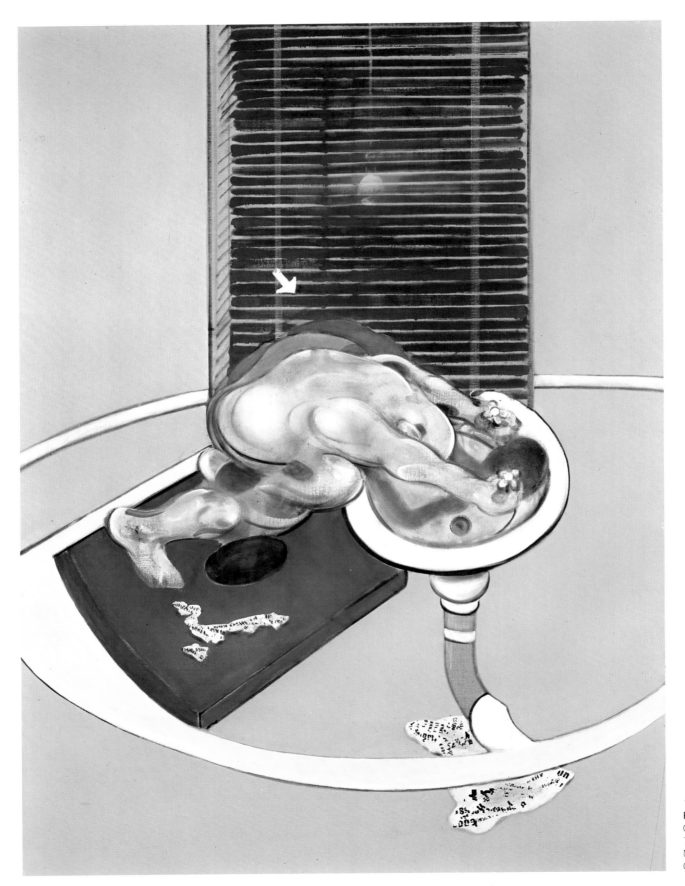

**104**
**Figure at a Washbasin.** 1976.
Oil on canvas,
78×58 in./198×147.5 cm.
Museo de Arte Contemporáneo,
Caracas.

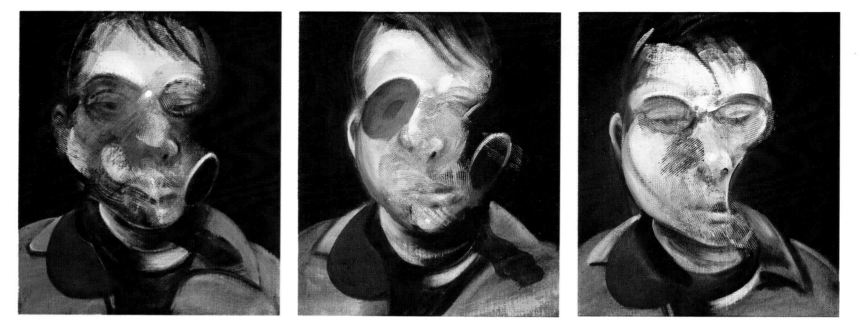

106
**Three Studies for Self-Portrait.** 1976.
Small triptych.
Oil on canvas,
each panel 14 × 12 in./35.5 × 30.5 cm.
Collection H. Thyssen-Bornemisza, Lugano.

107
**Portrait of Michel Leiris.** 1976.
Oil on canvas,
14 × 12 in./35.5 × 30.5 cm.
Collection Michel Leiris, Paris.

**108**
**Triptych.** 1974-77.
Oil and pastel on canvas,
each panel 78 × 58 in./198 × 147.5 cm.
Property of the Artist.

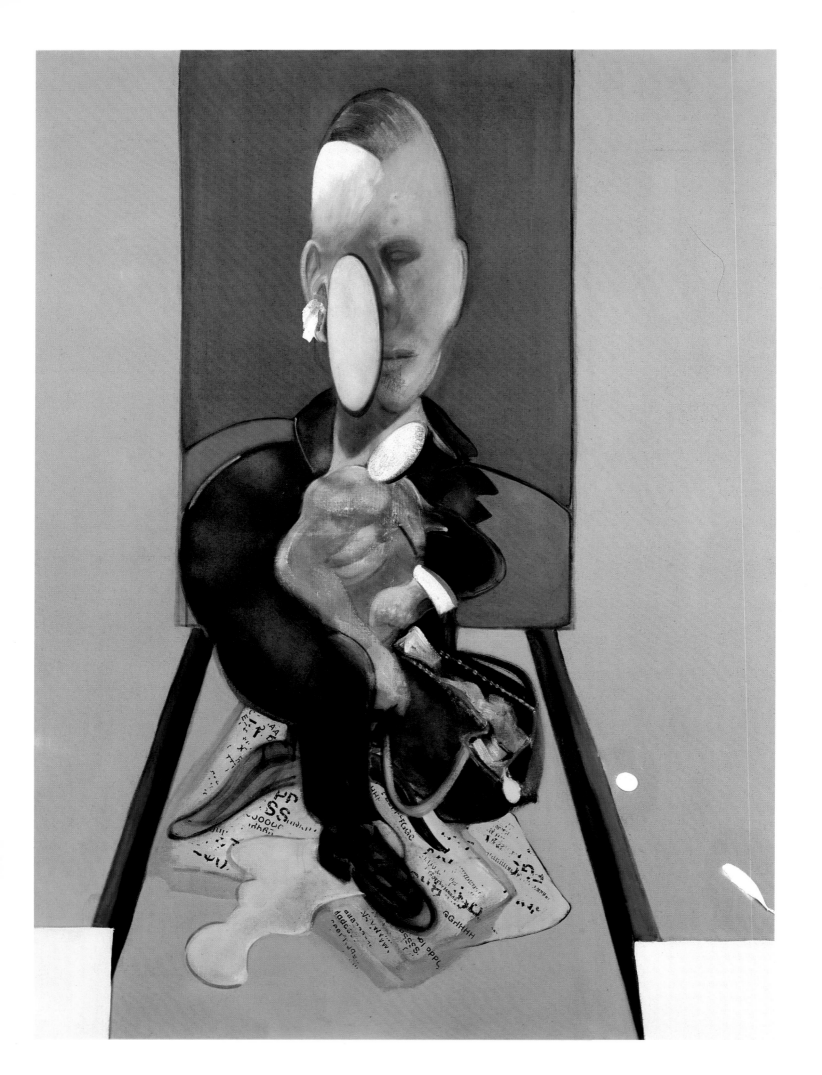

**109**
**Triptych.** 1976.
Oil and pastel on canvas,
each panel 78 × 58 in./198 × 147.5 cm.
Private collection, France.

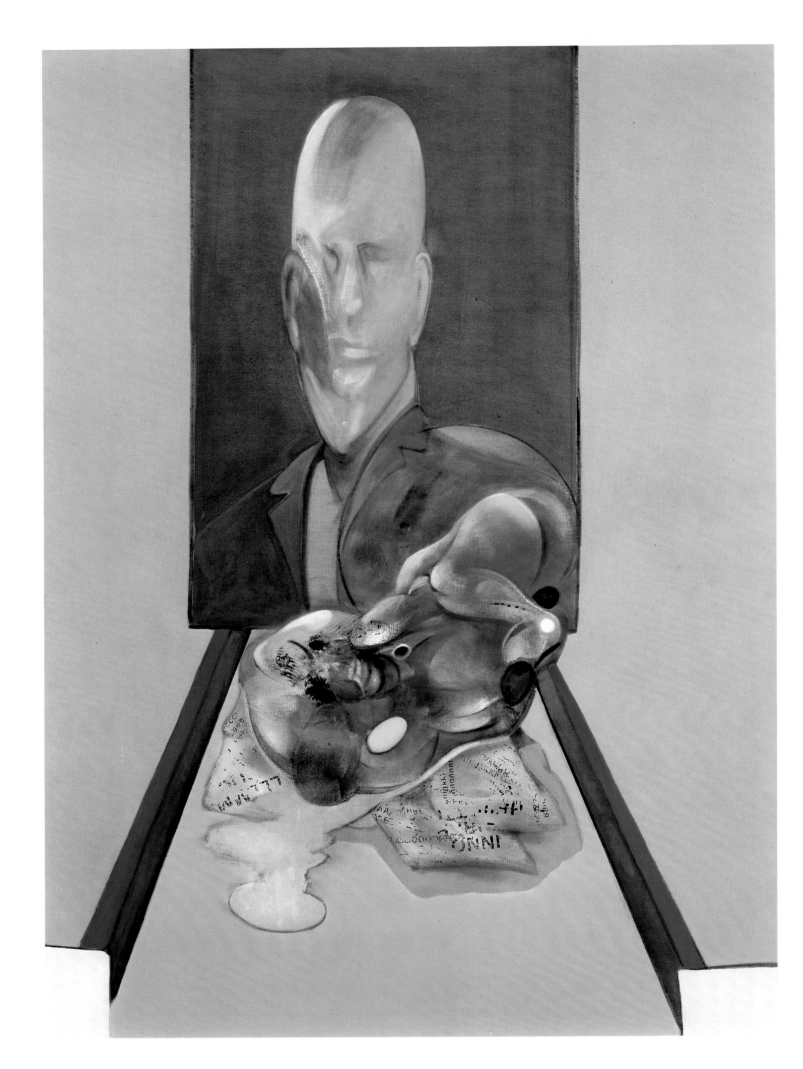

110
**Figure Writing Reflected in a Mirror.** 1976.
Oil on canvas,
78 × 58 in./198 × 147.5 cm.
Private collection, Paris.

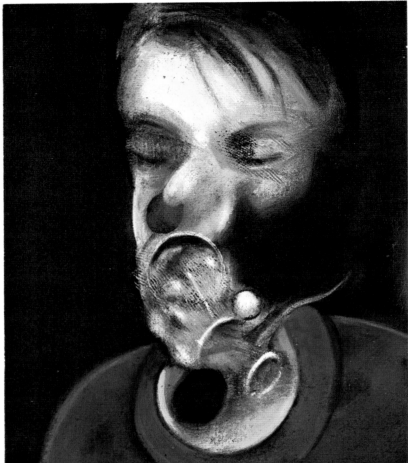

111
**Two Studies for Self-Portrait.** 1977.
Diptych.
Oil on canvas,
each panel 14 × 12 in./35.5 × 30.5 cm.
Private collection.

**112**
**Seated Figure.** 1977.
Oil on canvas,
78 × 58 in./198 × 147.5 cm.
Mrs. Susan Lloyd, Nassau.

113
**Study for Portrait.** 1977.
Oil on canvas,
78 × 58 in./198 × 147.5 cm.
Private collection, Monaco.

**114**
**Self-Portrait.** 1978.
Oil on canvas,
78 × 58 in./198 × 147.5 cm.
Private collection.

 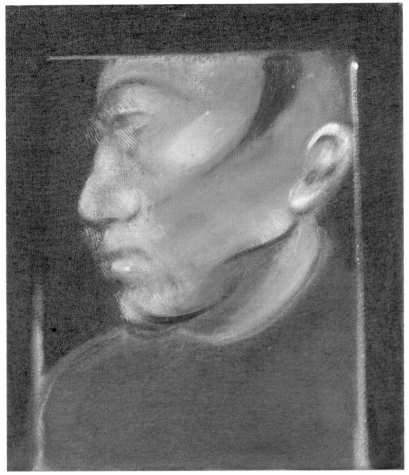

115
Two Studies for Portrait of
Richard Chopping. 1978.
Diptych.
Oil on canvas,
each panel 14 × 12 in./35.5 × 30.5 cm.
Private collection, Paris.

116
Study for Portrait (Michel Leiris). 1978.
Oil on canvas,
14 × 12 in./35.5 × 30.5 cm.
Collection Michel Leiris, Paris.

117
**Seated Figure.** 1978.
Oil on canvas,
78 × 58 in./198 × 147.5 cm.
Private collection, Malibu.

**118**
**Landscape.** 1978.
Oil and pastel on canvas,
78 × 58 in./198 × 147.5 cm.
Private collection, Switzerland.

119
**Figure in Movement.** 1978.
Oil and pastel on canvas,
78 × 58 in./198 × 147.5 cm.
Private collection, Los Angeles.

**120**
**Painting.** 1978.
Oil on canvas,
78 × 58 in./198 × 147.5 cm.
Private collection, Monaco.

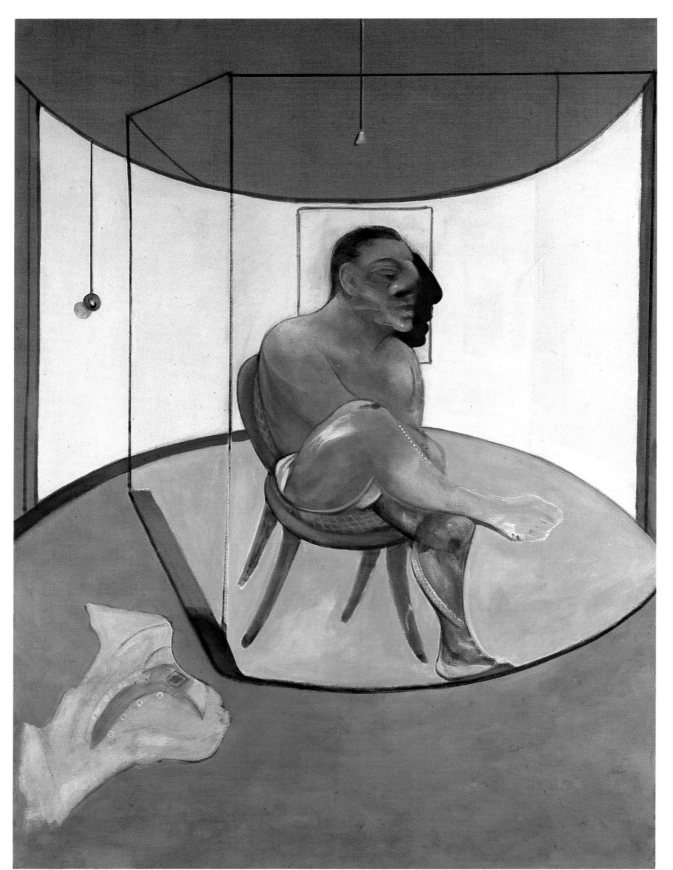

121
**Study for Portrait.** 1978.
Oil on canvas,
78 × 58 in./198 × 147.5 cm.
Private collection, Hartford, Conn.

122
**Jet of Water.** 1979.
Oil on canvas,
78 × 58 in./198 × 147.5 cm.
Private collection, New York.

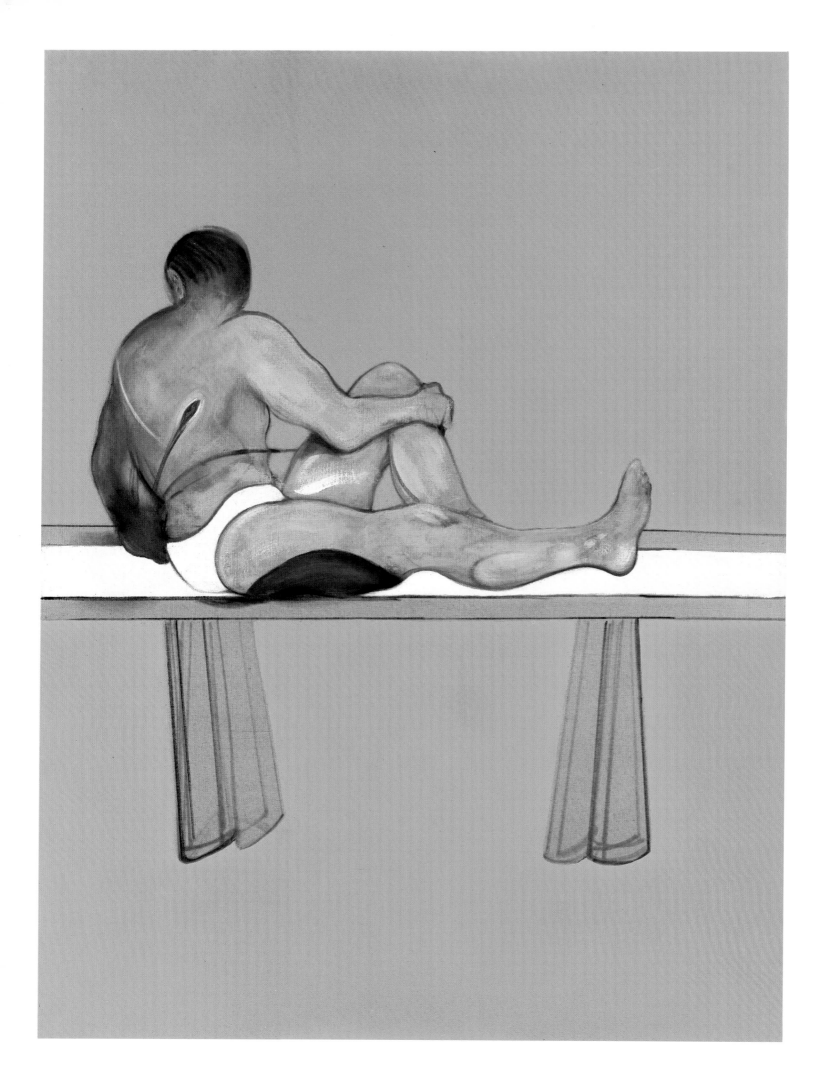

123
**Triptych - Studies of the Human Body.** 1979.
Oil on canvas,
each panel 78 × 58 in./198 × 147.5 cm.
Sutton Place Heritage Trust Ltd.

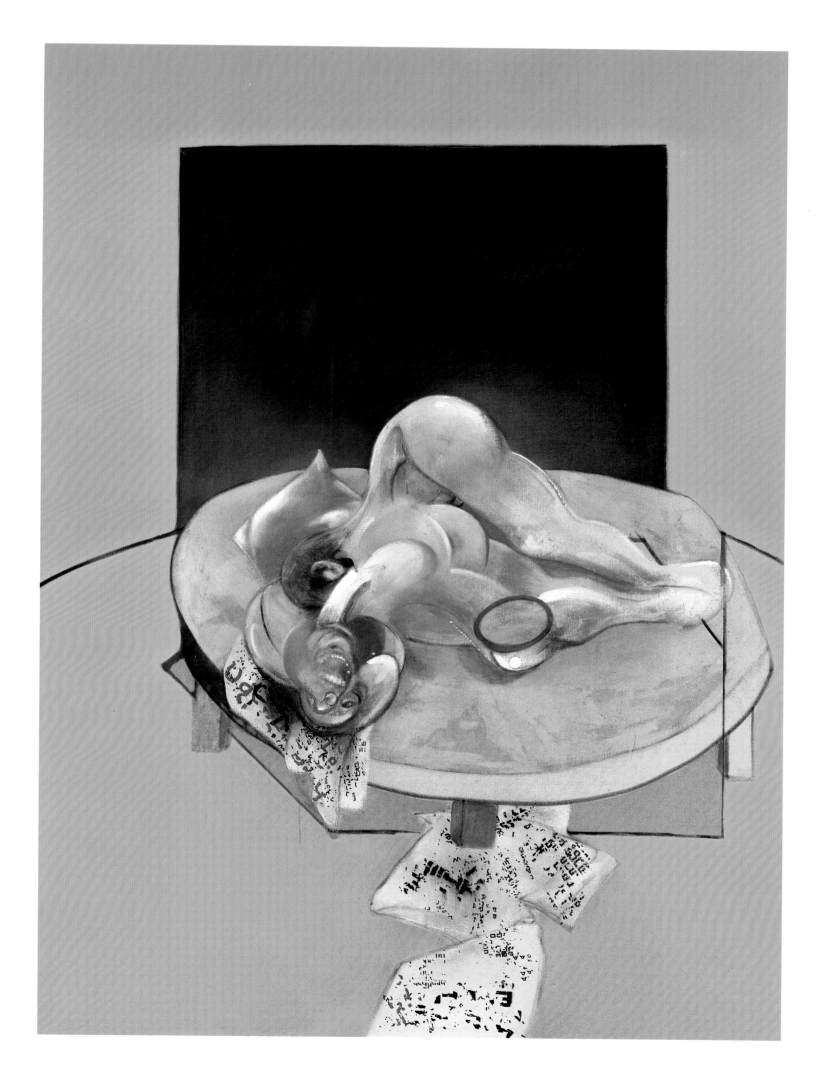

124
**Two Seated Figures.** 1979.
Oil on canvas,
78 × 58 in./198 × 147.5 cm.
Collection Dr. Theodore
J. Edlich Jr., New York.

**125**
**Seated Figure.** 1979.
Oil on canvas,
78 × 58 in./198 × 147.5 cm.
Marlborough International Fine Art.

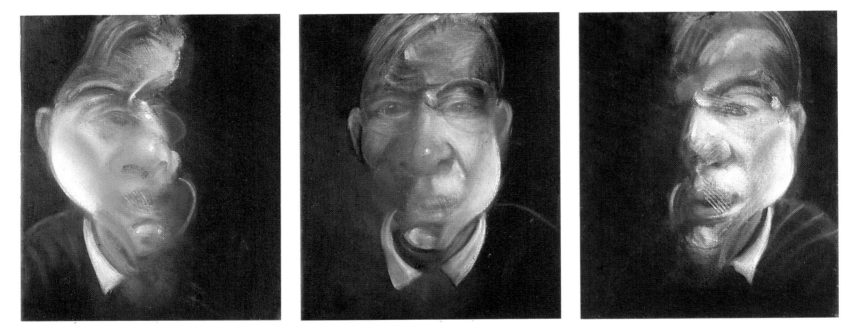

126
**Three Studies for Self-Portrait.** 1979.
Small triptych.
Oil on canvas,
each panel $14^{3}/_{4} \times 12^{1}/_{2}$ in./37.5 × 31.8 cm.
Private collection, Mexico.

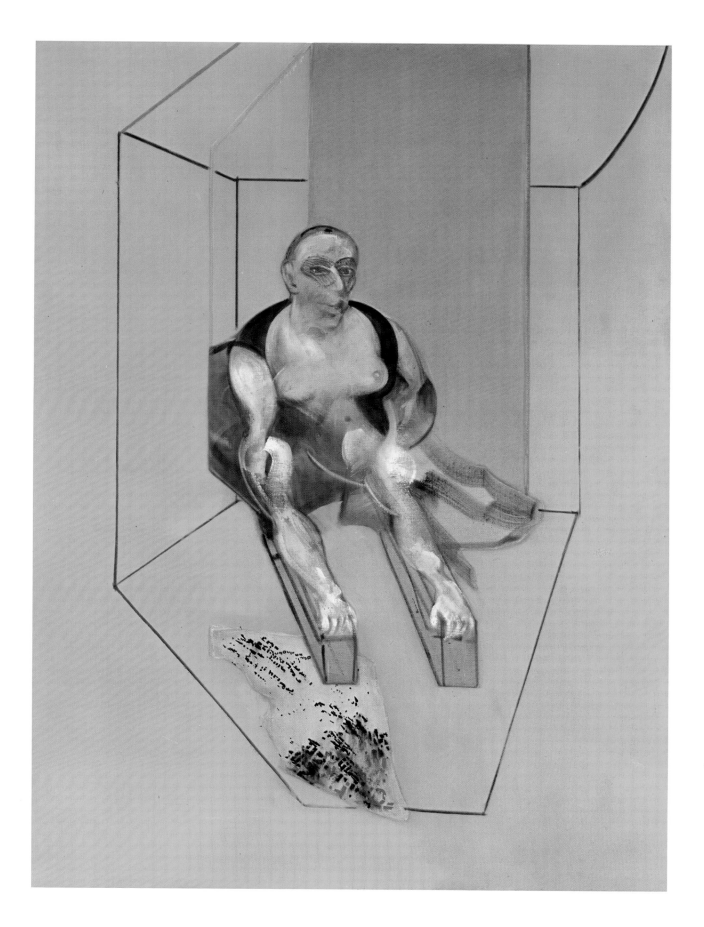

127
**Sphinx - Portrait of**
**Muriel Belcher.** 1979.
Oil on canvas,
78 × 58 in./198 × 147.5 cm.
Property of the Artist.

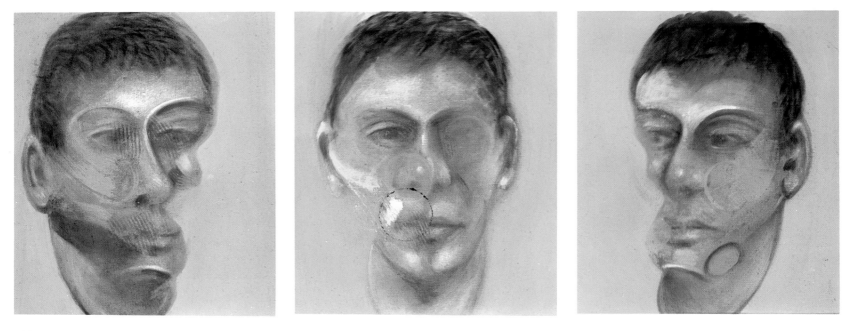

**128**
**Three Studies for a Portrait of John Edwards.** 1980.
Small triptych.
Oil on canvas,
each panel 14 × 12 in./35.5 × 30.5 cm.
Marlborough International Fine Art.

**129**
**The Wrestlers, after Muybridge.** 1980.
Oil and pastel on canvas,
78 × 58 in./198 × 147.5 cm.
Private collection, Tokyo.

**105**
**Figure in Movement.** 1976.
Oil on canvas,
78 × 58 in./198 × 147.5 cm.
Galerie Claude Bernard, Paris.

130
Study for Portrait with
Bird in Flight. 1980.
Oil on canvas,
78 × 58 in./198 × 147.5 cm.
Private collection, Toronto.

131
Carcase of Meat
and Bird of Prey. 1980.
Oil and pastel on canvas,
78 × 58 in./198 × 147.5 cm.
Collection Claude Bernard, Paris.

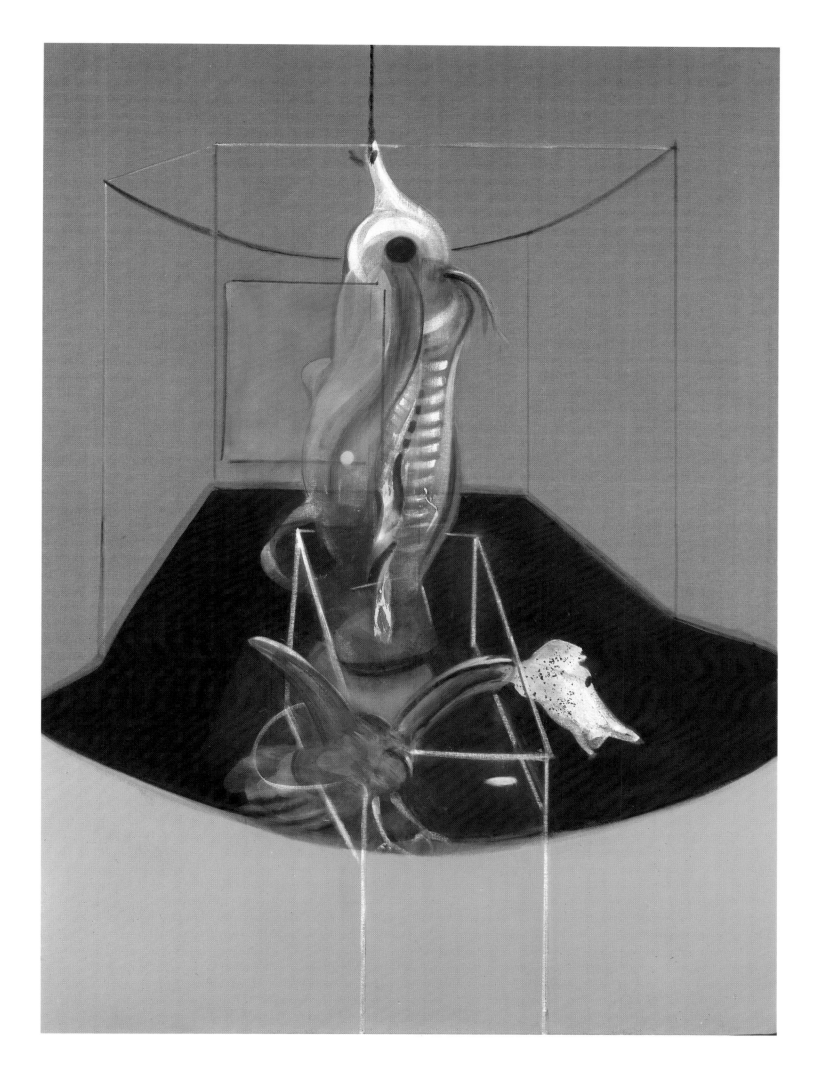

**132**
**Study for**
**Self-Portrait.**
1980.
Oil on canvas,
14 × 12 in./
35.5 × 30.5 cm.
Sutton Place
Heritage Trust Lt

**133**
**Study of a Man**
**Talking.** 1981.
Oil on canvas,
78 × 58 in./
198 × 147.5 cm.
Private collection,
Berne.

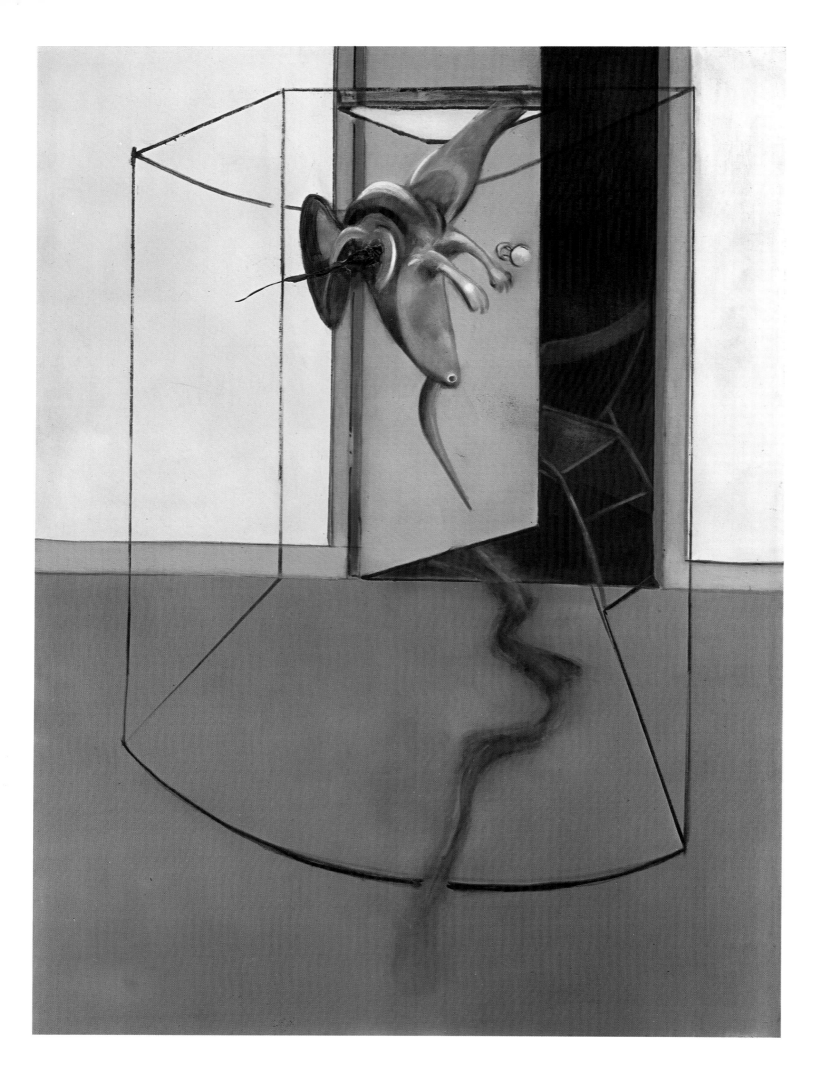

134
**Triptych.** 1981.
Inspired by the Oresteia of Aeschylus.
Oil on canvas,
each panel 78 × 58 in./198 × 147.5 cm.
Marlborough International Fine Art.

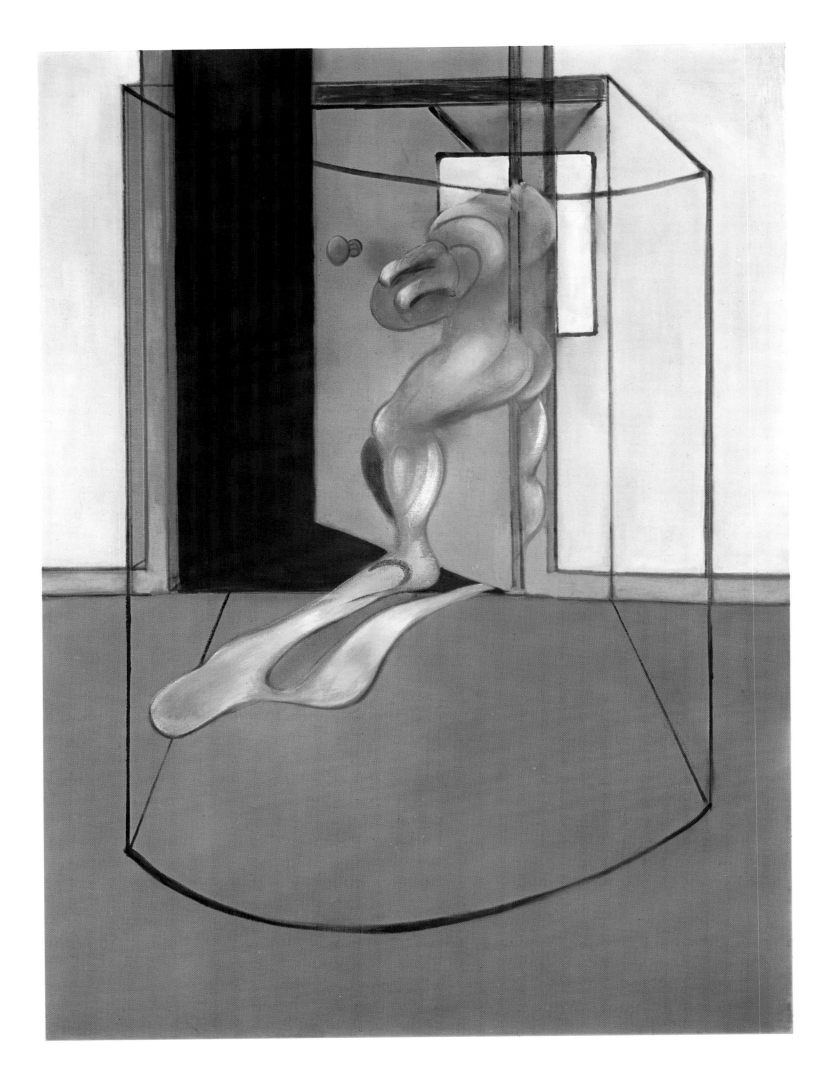

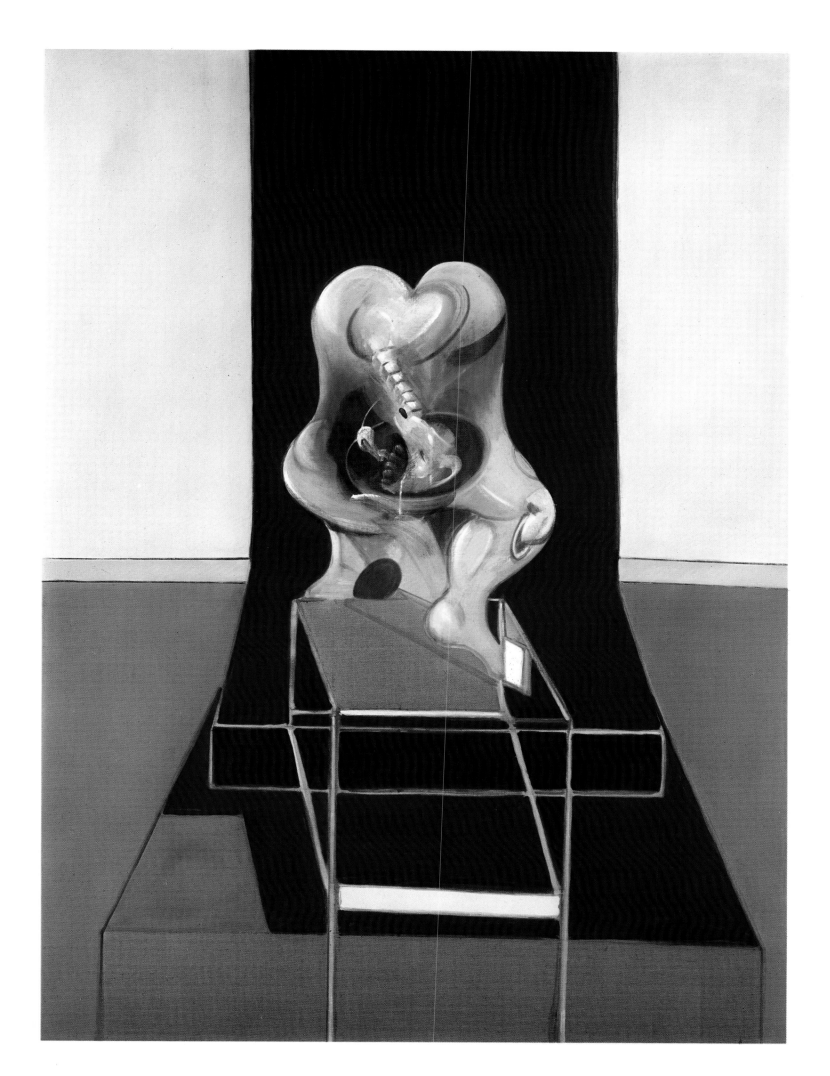

135
**Study for Portrait.** 1981.
Oil on canvas,
78 × 58 in./198 × 147.5 cm.
Marlborough International Fine Ar

136
**Sand Dune.** 1981.
Oil and pastel on canvas,
78 × 58 in./198 × 147.5 cm.
Marlborough International Fine Art.

137
**Study for Self-Portrait.** 1981.
Oil on canvas,
78 × 58 in./
198 × 147.5 cm.
Von der Heydt
Museum,
Wuppertal.

138
Study from the
Human Body.
1981.
Oil on canvas,
78×58 in./
198×147.5 cm.
Property
of the Artist.

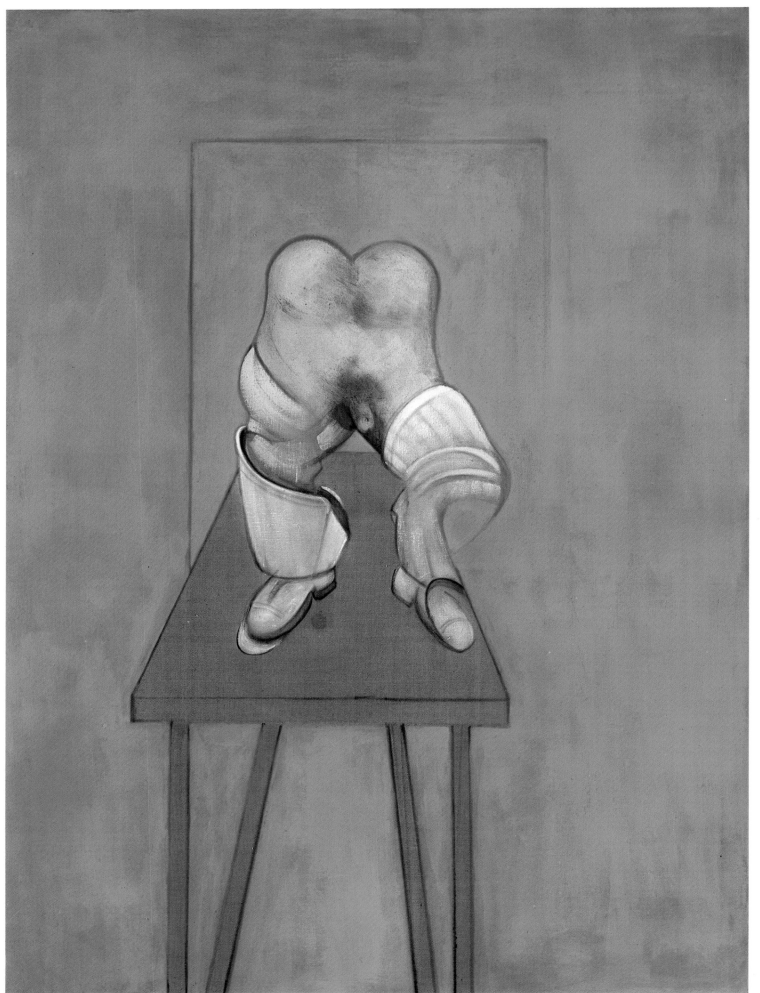

139
Study of the
Human Body.
1982.
Oil and pastel on
canvas,
78 × 58 in./
198 × 147.5 cm
Musée National
d'Art Moderne,
Centre Georges
Pompidou, Paris.

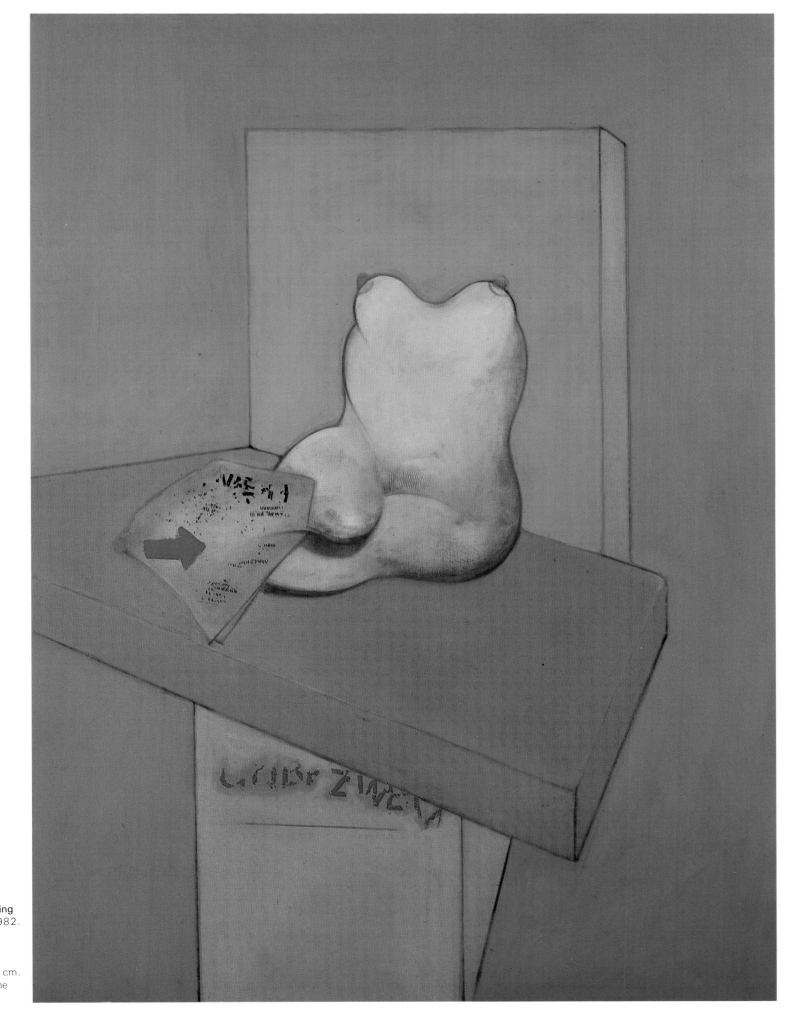

40
Study of the
Human Body
from a Drawing
by Ingres. 1982.
Oil and pastel
on canvas,
78 × 58 in./
198 × 147.5 cm.
Property of the
artist.

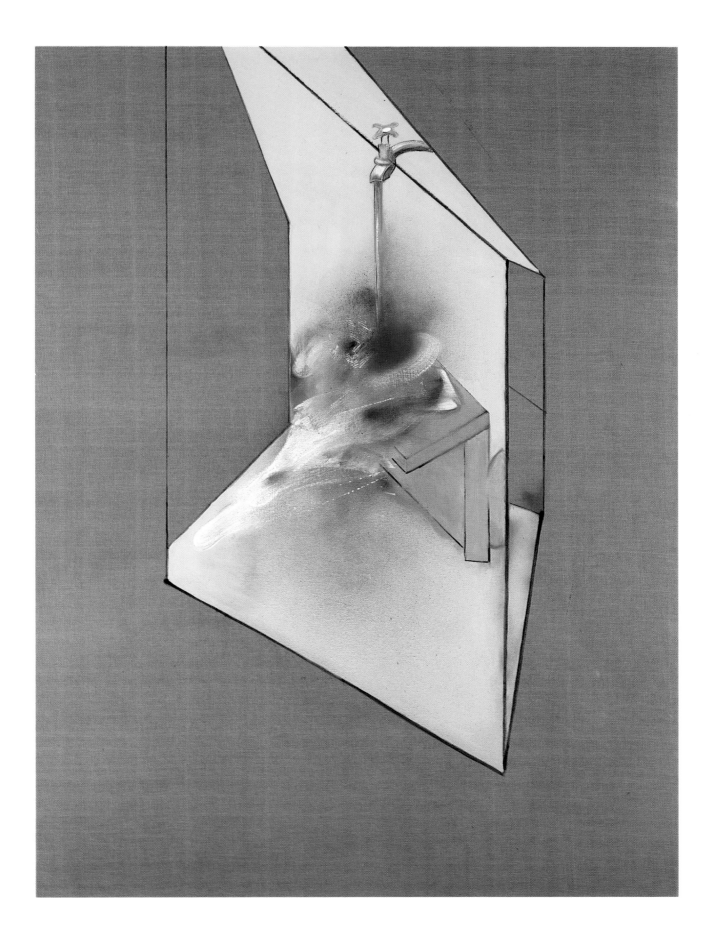

**141**
**Water from a Running Tap.**
1982.
Oil on canvas,
78 × 58 in./198 × 147.5 cm.
Private collection, Madrid.

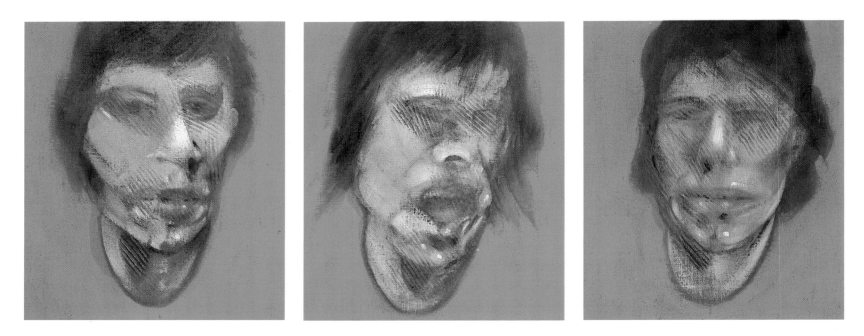

**142**
**Three Studies for a Portrait (Mick Jagger).** 1982.
Small triptych.
Oil and pastel on canvas,
each panel 14 × 12 in./35.5 × 30.5 cm.
Private collection, New York.

**143**
**Study for Self-Portrait.** 1982.
Oil on canvas,
78 × 58 in./198 × 147.5 cm.
Private collection, New York.

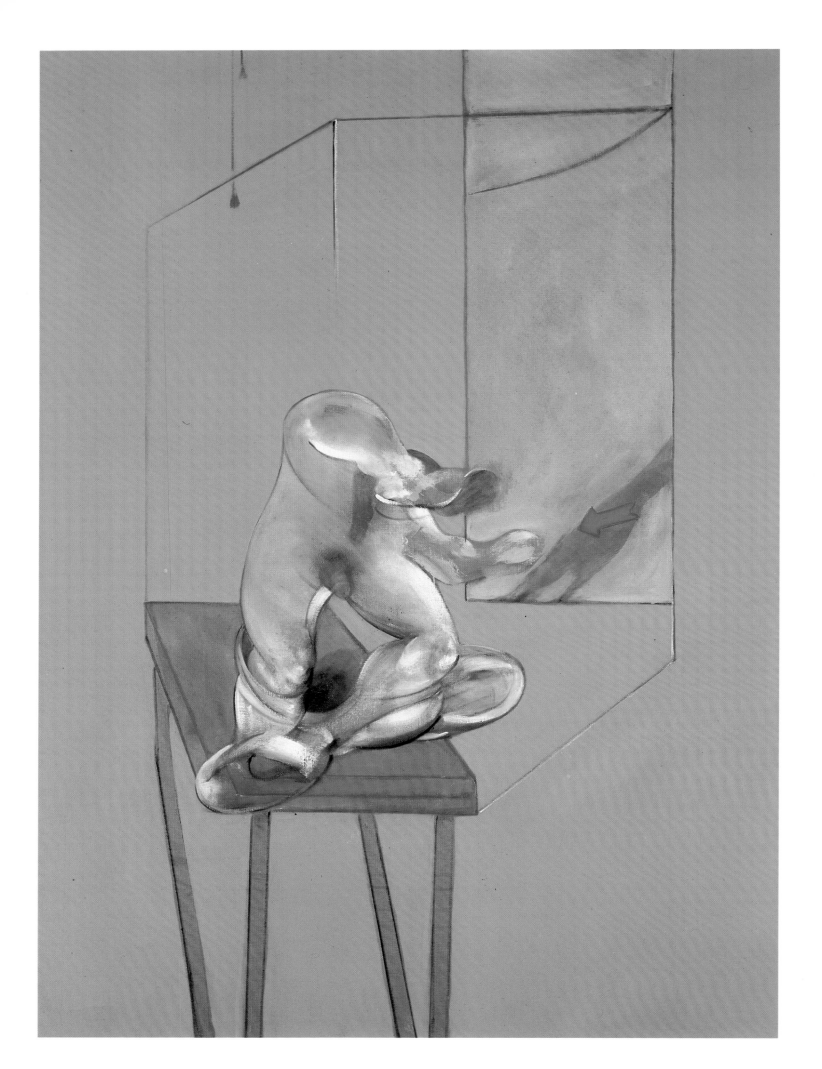

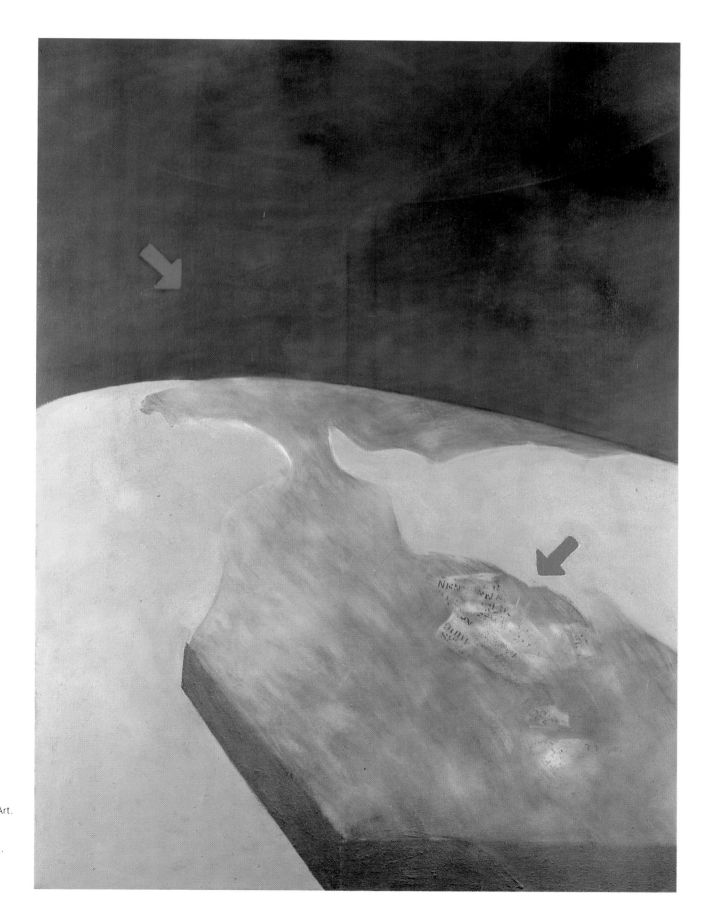

**144**
**Study of the Human Body.**
**Figure in Movement.** 1982.
Oil on canvas,
78 × 58 in./198 × 147.5 cm.
Marlborough International Fine Art.

**145**
**A Piece of Waste Land.** 1982.
Oil on canvas,
78 × 58 in./198 × 147.5 cm.
Property of the Artist.

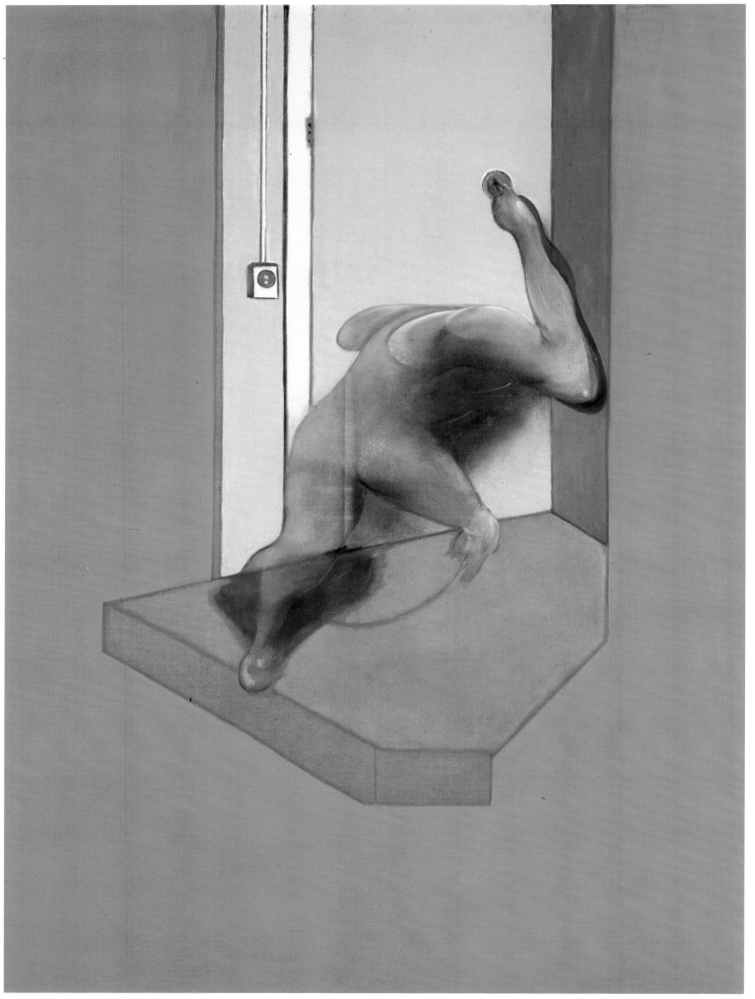

146
**Study of the
Human Body.**
1983.
Oil and pastel on
canvas,
78 × 58 in./
198 × 147.5 cm
Property of the
Artist.

# Francis Bacon

## FACE ET PROFIL

original text by Michel Leiris

Un Oreste dont viennent à peine d'être apaisées les Erinyes: un Hamlet rassemblant ses esprits après son affrontement avec le spectre; un Don Juan pas plus superman que son pleutre de valet mais bandant tous ses muscles pour braver l'enfer auquel le voue le Commandeur; un Maldoror mi-ange mi-ogre qui reprend souffle après avoir proféré le long blasphème de ses *Chants*; tantôt jovial tantôt songeur, un Falstaff que ses excès auraient laissé presque aussi jeune qu'à l'époque où il était page chez le duc de Norfolk; en prise directe sur nos jours diversement bouleversés, un flambeur au découpé élégamment moderne et que l'on croit surprendre à l'instant, déterminé par nulle horloge, où il joue son va-tout aux dés, aux cartes ou à la roulette... Coloré comme celui d'un empiriste anglais du XVIIIe siècle philosophant devant un verre de brandy ou de jerez, le visage imberbe, à la fois poupin et tourmenté, de Francis Bacon semble refléter l'étonnement qui fait ouvrir les yeux, l'opiniâtreté intelligente et, alliée à je ne sais quelle fureur secrète, une tendre détresse d'homme qui n'ignore pas qu'il fut jadis un enfant qu'à peu près n'importe quoi pouvait émerveiller. Virgule hasardeuse barrant obstinément le front, la mèche que n'omet aucun des portraits de lui-même qu'il a peints paraît être un emblème montrant que dans sa tête rien ne s'opère selon les normes paresseuses d'une voie toute tracée mais qu'il y a toujours suspens, brisure ou remise en question. Serait-ce un même refus des solutions en prêt-à-porter qui s'inscrirait dans l'allure un peu de guingois — nullement frontale à tout le moins — qu'on lui voit sur plusieurs photographies et qui, comme sa démarche qu'on croirait toujours sur le point de se faire danse, pourrait être l'indice d'une répugnance au tranquille équilibre des gens sous les pieds de qui le sol ne s'est jamais dérobé?

Contrastant avec la mise désinvolte mais toujours parfaitement nette de ce personnage impossible à réduire à une figure unique et qu'il faudrait aussi — oubliant tout romantisme — montrer sous son aspect bourreau de travail levé de bon matin quelle que soit la façon dont il a passé la nuit, le désordre de l'atelier londonien — un capharnaüm dans le bien peigné du quartier résidentiel où l'héberge une de ces *mews* qui sont d'anciennes écuries — semble tout naturellement, avec son sol jamais désencombré, appeler impérieusement, par son échevellement même, à la relative création d'ordre que sera symboliquement l'exécution du tableau et tout

à la fois constituer, pour l'œil de celui qui a laissé tant de choses s'accumuler (matériel de travail, photos qui traînent et s'abîment, etc.) dans le local où habituellement il dort et où non moins habituellement il peint, un équivalent à trois dimensions du fameux mur de Léonard de Vinci, porteur de suggestions multiples.

Qu'il rende compte de choses existantes ou procède essentiellement du jeu de l'imagination, l'art n'a-t-il pas pour fonction dernière de nous sauver du désastre en doublant le monde usuel d'un autre monde agencé au gré de notre esprit, selon un ordre intime qui, en tant que tel, tranche sur l'invraisemblable fouillis de la réalité ambiante? Et n'est-ce pas quelque chose d'analogue à des lieux bâtis, civilisés, dont l'ordonnance — quelque forme qu'elle prenne — tient en respect la sauvagerie environnante, que les arts plastiques paraissent destinés à fournir, comme producteurs d'images sur lesquelles le regard se fixe et qui, objets d'une autre essence que les innombrables éléments du monde extérieur, seront pour nous des sortes de points d'ancrage? Ainsi, l'artiste, si l'on admet que son jeu va plus loin qu'un simple divertissement, trouverait sa raison d'être dans l'existence même de ce chaos où nous sommes plongés, confusion dans laquelle il lui reviendrait de faire entendre son propre dire qui, pour ténu qu'il soit, sera du moins le sien (dit d'une voix proprement humaine et telle que nos créations expressément utilitaires ne peuvent nous en renvoyer l'écho). Difficile à décrire dans son apparence qu'aucun schéma rigide ne saurait caractériser, Francis Bacon aurait-il, en tant que peintre qui se veut rien que tel et adepte moins d'un art que d'un jeu qui ne comporte aucun message, une voix au timbre moins rebelle à la définition?

Comme si elle avait sa vie à elle et constituait une réalité neuve au lieu de n'être qu'un simulacre, une allusion indirecte ou bien un arrangement dûment équilibré (sans plus de tranchant qu'une pure ornementation), ce qui, dans une toile de Francis Bacon, quels que soient les éléments mis en œuvre et même quand son thème la situe sur le plan du mythe plutôt que sur celui du quotidien, est appréhendé sur-le-champ et s'impose sans le moindre détour, indépendamment de tout jugement d'adhésion ou de refus, c'est, étrangère à quoi que ce soit qui de près ou de loin relèverait d'une théologie, l'espèce de *présence réelle* à laquelle atteignent les figures qui animent de pareilles œuvres. Par leur intermédiaire, en effet, le spectateur sans idées préconçues touche à un ordre de réalité chair et sang qui n'est pas sans rapport avec ce qu'un acte paroxystique tel que l'amour physique fait toucher dans la vie ordinaire. De quelle folle ambiguïté, chatoiement fascinant, se pare cette présence réelle, qui se donne à goûter voluptueusement mais, pour savoureux qu'en soit le véhicule pictural, est d'une telle intensité que d'aucuns, rebutés peut-être par semblable brûlure, ne verront là que hideur!

Loin de n'agir qu'à fleur de peau et par leur seul pittoresque, les œuvres de Francis Bacon ne laissent pas de préoccuper, d'imprégner en bien ou en mal même une fois passé le moment toujours surprenant à quelque degré de la saisie, vertu qui (d'évidence) témoigne de leur haute valeur. Qu'est-ce, en effet, qu'une œuvre peinte qui ne possède pas la capacité d'obséder et qui, après un temps plus ou moins long de commerce avec nous, apparaît comme guère plus qu'un accident rompant la monotonie du mur auquel elle est accrochée? Seules existent véritablement, ont une pleine réalité celles qui exercent sur nous une emprise persistante — comme en vérité le peuvent aussi, question de qualité et non pas de durée, des choses aussi éphémères qu'un chant, une performance d'acteur ou une danse — et interviennent dans nos façons ultérieures de sentir et de penser au lieu de nous avoir seulement frappés d'une impression, vive peut-être mais qui, nous émouvant sans rien changer à notre façon affective de prendre le monde en compte, ne nous portait pas au-delà des frontières du dilettantisme.

Ce que Francis Bacon montre dans la plupart de ses tableaux, à quelque phase de son évolution qu'ils appartiennent, ce sont — compte non tenu de ce qui n'y entre qu'à titre d'accessoire ou d'élément de décor — des figurations de personnages vivants ou de choses généralement banales dotées, au moins en apparence, d'une certaine véracité d'images en référence directe avec des expériences vécues par le canal des sens ou, plus largement, par celui de la sensibilité mais dont il est manifeste que, loin d'être des reflets du monde ambiant comme ceux que nous offre la photographie, elles résultent d'un emploi tout à fait libre des moyens artisanaux de la peinture, semblants dont pourtant la nature de fictions peintes tend à se faire oublier et qui existent plus forte-

ment que comme simples représentations (sont, nous semble-t-il, des êtres d'un type particulier et non des simulacres dénués de toute vie propre). En d'autres termes, on pourrait dire que chez Francis Bacon le but essentiel est moins d'exécuter un tableau qui sera un objet digne d'être regardé que de faire s'affirmer quelques réalités sur la toile prise pour théâtre d'opérations. En cela cet artiste — qui sans vaine volonté de modernisme se situe indubitablement, par son style autant que par les éléments qu'il met en jeu, dans la seconde moitié de notre siècle — se différencie non seulement des surréalistes (qui, férus de rêve et d'invention d'ordre fantasmatique, font du tableau un écran récepteur de projections hautement imaginaires) mais des cubistes (pour qui le tableau, transposition radicale d'un motif vrai ou censé tel, valait comme composition fortement structurée où n'entre aucun truquage optique) et aussi bien de leurs grands prédécesseurs les impressionnistes (dont les tableaux étaient fenêtres ouvertes ou trous de serrure flattant l'œil avec tel fragment lumineux ou tamisé de quotidien).

S'abstenant de faire appel soit à des éclairages troublants (qui inclineraient son travail vers un expressionnisme, alors qu'il récuse catégoriquement cette tendance et, réaliste dédaigneux de toute emphase comme de toute visée dramatique ou satirique, cherche sans en rajouter à traduire ses sensations aussi persuasivement que possible), soit à de délicats ou brillants jeux visuels (à la manière impressionniste), Francis Bacon place généralement ce dont il traite sous une dure lumière fixe d'électricité ou, parfois, de net soleil que ne nuance rien qui relèverait de la météorologie, tout se passant en somme dans la crudité de midi — sommet du jour et *heure de vérité* — ou celle de ce qu'en langage de théâtre on appellerait *pleins feux*. Est-il abusif d'en déduire que, dans toutes ses toiles, cet homme aux facettes multiples tient à jouer cartes sur table et, rebelle aux atermoiements non moins qu'aux finesses surannées, à payer rubis sur l'ongle, en cette ''immédiateté'' qu'il veut bien reconnaître à certaines de ses œuvres, comme il le dit à l'historien d'art David Sylvester dans l'un de leurs entretiens rédigés d'après de longs enregistrements et aujourd'hui au nombre de sept (plus un inédit) mais où les problèmes posés sont discutés avec tant d'acharnement à dissiper toute équivoque qu'un tel dialogue pourrait s'étendre à l'infini, documents exemplaires montrant combien peu Francis Bacon se soucie de laisser coquettement planer une ombre sur son travail et quelle rare rectitude de vue va chez lui de pair avec un désordre apparent? Immédiateté, dirai-je, qui est non seulement soudaineté de l'effet produit mais roide mise au pied du mur où le spectateur se voit bousculé sans pitié, à l'égal (semble-t-il) de l'auteur lui-même, toujours en cause profondément dans ce qu'il peint, tout comme on le voit directement impliqué dans les réponses sans ambages qu'il apporte à l'implacable questionnaire d'un inquisiteur obstiné et sagace.

L'espace où nous respirons, ici même, le temps dans lequel, maintenant, nous vivons, c'est ce qu'à peu d'exceptions près l'on trouve dans les toiles de Francis Bacon, toiles qui semblent viser à exprimer immédiatement quelque chose d'immédiat et dont il ne suffira pas de dire que très généralement elles sont exemptes de tout exotisme et de tout archaïsme, échappant seuls à cette règle le *Paysage au rhinocéros* de 1952 (basé sur une photographie provenant d'Afrique équatoriale et finalement détruit comme Francis Bacon l'a fait de nombre de ses tableaux), l'*Homme portant un enfant* (souvenir 1956 d'un long séjour à Tanger), les *Papes* (inspirés entre 1949 et 1952 par le célèbre *Innocent X* de Velázquez) et, anachroniques en quelque mesure, les portraits de Van Gogh (1957) dont certains de facture quelque peu fauviste, presque mais point absolument nos contemporains. Entre la plupart des tableaux de Francis Bacon — artiste dont je voudrais marquer ici à tout le moins la singularité — et ceux qui les regardent, la proximité est, en effet, plus grande que si dans leurs thèmes il y avait, sans plus, absence d'éloignement spatial ou temporel. Bien que pareilles œuvres ne tiennent nullement du trompe-l'œil (ersatz qui d'ailleurs ne fait pas sérieusement illusion) et que leur auteur procède en sorte qu'elles soient d'authentiques créations aussi distinctes de l'abstrait que de ce qu'il nomme dépréciativement ''illustratif'', l'on pourrait dire à leur propos que c'est *comme si on y était,* voire même qu'*on y est* (qu'on est dans le tableau et pas seulement devant), formule indiquant une pleine participation et qui, en ce sens, va plus loin qu'un *ça est* dans lequel le présent serait substitué au passé de la formule à l'emporte-pièce que, dans le livre effectivement éclairant qu'est *La Chambre claire,* Roland Barthes appliquait à la photographie: le "ça a été" exprimant que celle-ci, dont la

vocation paradoxale est d'agir moins en tant que présentation sans recul ni artifice qu'en tant que témoignage rétrospectif comme l'est nécessairement un témoignage, atteste péremptoirement que quelque chose a existé ou s'est produit.

Dans maintes toiles de Francis Bacon, celles qui — point de vue, il va de soi, subjectif — me semblent les plus typiques, soit celles de la pleine maturité de cet artiste qui, n'ayant jamais étudié dans aucune académie, s'est, presque littéralement à la force du poignet, construit son métier en autodidacte, c'est en un lieu décrit (approximativement) selon les règles traditionnelles de la perspective et, de ce fait, crédible que les choses nous sont montrées. Toutes proches, on les dirait grandeur nature et elles semblent placées sur un sol qui serait le nôtre, en apparence prolongement de celui sur lequel nous nous tenons face au tableau. C'est comme si, intégrés et non en position de spectateur pur, nous avions affaire directement à ces choses. En de tels tableaux — qui ont bien leur géométrie, mais une géométrie si l'on peut dire périphérique (ne concernant que les entours) au lieu d'affecter les figures mêmes, traitées trop librement pour être réductibles à des structures simples — la construction d'ensemble répond moins à une visée décorative, voire proprement plastique, qu'à des exigences de mise en page, mise en scène, mise en valeur — cela côté œuvre à échafauder mais, côté spectateur dont l'œil et l'esprit sont frappés, expressément mise en présence. Généralement clos et exigu, l'espace du tableau — milieu qui n'apparaît ni comme un substitut ni comme un modèle réduit mais comme une réplique du nôtre — semble constituer — qu'il s'agisse d'une chambre sans personnalité ou, plus vaste, d'un endroit de plein air au demeurant des plus quelconques — une espèce de boîte dans laquelle, idéalement, sera inclus le spectateur, fictivement situé dans le lieu même où, apparemment à son échelle, la chose lui est montrée et, gratifié ainsi d'un rôle moins anodin que celui du spectateur cloué à son fauteuil, promu au rang de voyeur, assistant de plain-pied au semblant de scène sans anecdote racontable qui lui est proposé et pris au piège d'un espace le plus souvent fermé sur lui-même mais toujours ouvert à lui qui, en imagination, y pénètre comme tout le dispositif paraît établi pour l'y inviter.

Notre espace, donc, mais aussi notre temps. Outre qu'on croirait y retrouver un aspect de la biographie de l'artiste qui, avant que la vocation de peintre ne survienne en lui (de même qu'on voit, dirait-on, la peinture survenir dans la froide structure de pareilles toiles), avait été quelque temps dessinateur d'ameublement, nombre d'œuvres de Francis Bacon sont en effet conçues comme si leur actualité devait être rendue évidente. Non seulement modernité quant aux costumes que portent les personnages et quant aux meubles (jamais autres que fonctionnels) dont ils sont les usagers, mais autres accessoires empruntés à notre exacte époque: ampoules et commutateurs électriques, carpettes, parapluies, rasoirs de sûreté, lavabos et sièges de W.C., téléphones, appareils photo, journaux au texte illisible (qui, déchirés et traînant à terre, suggèrent par ailleurs un désordre analogue à celui qui règne positivement dans l'atelier de l'artiste), cigarettes à demi consumées (comme pour souligner aussi, par cette référence à une minute précise, l'aspect pris sur le vif, flagrant délit, épiphanie joycienne, qu'a le tableau), flèches qui semblent provenir de panneaux signalétiques ou faire partie de schémas indicateurs de mouvement comme pourrait en contenir tel ouvrage de technologie, etc. Tout cela traité moins en style proprement pictural qu'en style de stricte information (sans esthétisation de l'objet fabriqué comme il est courant chez Fernand Léger ou comme, en fait, Man Ray y tend plus ou moins avec ses rayographes). De même que, par d'autres moyens, l'espace du tableau est donné pour notre espace à nous qui regardons, il semble que Francis Bacon tienne à clairement signifier que ce qu'il cherche à pourvoir d'une apparence de vie se trouve situé — comme l'est par définition toute chose authentiquement vivante — dans un temps qui ne saurait être que le nôtre. La vêture (d'une actualité banale) ou la nudité (nullement académique) des personnages de Francis Bacon pourrait être, en cet instant, celle de lui l'auteur ou celle de nous les spectateurs.

Immédiate à un double titre (agissant immédiatement et parlant presque toujours de choses d'ici et de maintenant), la peinture de Francis Bacon n'est, de surcroît, porteuse d'aucun message — ce qu'il affirme catégoriquement dès l'un de ses premiers entretiens avec David Sylvester tout comme il récuse la qualification, assurément hâtive, d'expressionniste. Ne doit-on pas admettre que son propos est de pratiquer une peinture sans distance aucune, si l'on peut dire? De même qu'un tel art exclut l'éloignement aussi bien dans l'espace que

dans le temps, il ne s'accommode pas de cette distance d'un autre ordre qu'on pourrait nommer la distance de réflexion, soit celle qui est le propre d'un art que l'on ne saisira totalement que grâce à un certain travail de la pensée et, en quelque mesure, à terme, puisqu'il procède par allusion appelant interprétation plus ou moins lente et que son action, loin d'opérer *en foudre*, ne le fait que de manière tant soit peu différée, après un cheminement qui évidemment en affaiblit l'impact alors même qu'il en accroîtrait la résonance.

Bien que tant par sa facture que par son iconographie la peinture de Francis Bacon soit dépourvue d'austérité, l'on peut à son propos parler de dépouillement, indiquant par là à quel point elle fait fi des symboles comme de tout ce qui renverrait soit à des réminiscences folkloriques, soit à des prestiges étrangers à nos habituels entours. Dépouillement qui, au fond, s'accorde avec celui du jeu, comme on peut l'attendre de quelqu'un qui ne se contente pas d'être, dans la vie, un joueur (fervent surtout du jeu rapide et complètement aléatoire qu'est la roulette) mais estime que de nos jours la peinture, privée de toute fonction sacralisante, ne peut plus être qu'un jeu (ce qui, l'on ne saurait en disconvenir, est une vue des plus discutables puisque c'est oublier qu'un rôle éducateur peut encore lui être assigné, fût-ce malencontreusement). De même que l'art comme le conçoit Francis Bacon (un art démystifié, purgé qu'il est de tout halo religieux comme de toute dimension morale, ce qui revient presque au même, et par là profondément réaliste jusque dans les cas, ceux-là plus rares, où l'habitué du bar de cette Muriel Belcher aujourd'hui défunte qu'il a plusieurs fois portraiturée ne cherche pas à rendre compte d'une réalité extérieure, mais à faire réel, à donner corps indubitablement à ce qui n'est qu'intérieur et n'existe que pour lui), le jeu — activité sans justification mais pour laquelle on peut pourtant se passionner à mort — n'est-il pas essentiellement chose de l'immédiateté, valable sur le moment (non selon une finalité qui mettrait en cause l'ultérieur) et dénué de tout sens hormis sa pratique même?

Si, comme il le dit, l'art ne peut plus, de nos jours, être qu'un jeu (idée bien différente de l'idée d'*art pour l'art* car elle n'implique aucune valorisation particulière qui à défaut d'art sanctifiant tendrait à sanctifier l'art lui-même), en quoi Francis Bacon, parfait laïc qui ne croit à nulle transcendance, dépasse-t-il le divertissement pur, dans ce jeu dont il paraît plus fou encore que des classiques jeux de hasard?

A l'inverse de cet autre meneur d'un très grand jeu, Picasso, qui semble s'être plu à expérimenter les manières les plus diverses de signifier et a ainsi remis en question tout le langage pictural, Francis Bacon — proche en cela de son contemporain Alberto Giacometti — paraît s'être efforcé de figurer de façon aussi juste et efficace que possible. Pour lui, le jeu ne consiste pas tellement à inventer des signes, il est avant tout une joute entre l'artiste et ce que celui-ci entend signifier, lutte qui, interaction entre contingence du motif et image que l'on trace en se fiant aux pulsions qui subjectivement nous animent, engendre cette "tension" que Francis Bacon réclame et qui, selon lui, fait forcément défaut aux œuvres non figuratives.

Hormis quelques grandes compositions d'ordre indubitablement tragique, qui généralement ont pris la forme aujourd'hui peu commune de triptyques, et un petit nombre de tableaux dont le motif appartient certes à la nature mais est extérieur à l'humanité (animaux, rarissimes paysages, herbe, jet d'eau, tourbillon de sable), le thème privilégié de Francis Bacon c'est, de toute évidence, la réalité vivante d'un être humain. A ce point de vue, il est remarquable que, dans son œuvre pourtant assez varié, ne figure aucune nature morte — sauf toutefois, outre l'*Étude pour une figure* (1945-1946) qui se réduit à un pardessus plié, un chapeau posé et un monceau de fleurs, le volet central, où s'entrebâille un sac de voyage, du triptyque de 1967 dérivé sans filiation visible du "mélodrame aristophanesque" de T. S. Eliot, *Sweeney agonistes* —, remarquable également que même l'eau ou le sable, quand il les met en jeu, apparaissent animés d'un mouvement violent — jet puissant ou tourbillon — qui leur confère un semblant de vie, cette vie que Francis Bacon, soit qu'il transcrive soit qu'il invente, semble chercher par-dessus tout à exprimer, plutôt qu'il ne s'attache à restituer, en les refondant, les formes que le motif réel ou imaginaire revêt et à les pourvoir, éventuellement, d'un sens. Sans parler de la façon dont y sont présentées les figures, n'est-ce pas, du reste, au rythme de la vie que fait songer la structure générale de ceux des tableaux de Francis Bacon que j'oserai dire les plus baconiens? De même que dans la vie les temps forts (où l'aventure se noue) tranchent sur la platitude du train quotidien, les fonds de ces tableaux — telles des eaux calmes — laissent ici et là place à des foyers où la peinture se fait virulente, endroits dont on croirait qu'ils sont, dans la froideur du décor environnant, des brèches où le feu sacré du peintre, ici non domestiqué, brûle en toute liberté. A le voir jouer sur une pareille opposition — ordre clairement établi encadrant un désordre — on est fondé à penser que Francis Bacon a peu à peu découvert, par son intuition d'artiste plus que par des voies logiques, qu'une différence de potentiel est nécessaire pour que le courant passe et que surgisse quelque chose qui ressemble à la vie.

Chez Francis Bacon la toile a donc ses parties bouillantes, où règne une effervescence, en opposition avec ses parties neutres, où il ne se passe rien. Défis à la saine mesure, ces parties, que l'on pourrait comparer à ce que sont, dans la musique de jazz, des *breaks* se greffant sur la trame régulièrement cadencée — en termes plus classiques, parties fougueuses ou, si l'on veut, dionysiaques opposées à des parties calmes ou apolliniennes — seraient, si romantiquement on se réfère au poète flamme et cristal Stéphane Mallarmé qui en passant par le noir et blanc d'un agencement typographique non sans rapport avec celui des titres de journaux donna une dimension hautement métaphysique à un jeu d'absolu hasard, celles où en ouragan se lancent les dés (se joue le grand jeu), les autres n'étant guère plus que *neutralité identique du gouffre* et ne faisant que composer le lieu où quelques présences se seront picturalement manifestées comme pour contrer la formule dénonciatrice d'inanité *rien n'aura eu lieu que le lieu*. Un lieu qui, en l'espèce, est certes pratiquement nul mais doit être perçu comme lieu (la peinture étant essentiellement affaire de perception sensorielle directe) et exige donc d'être posé clairement, encore qu'en fait il reste assez peu qualifié pour apparaître, lui qui se borne à héberger le ou les personnages qui animent le tableau, comme une sorte d'annexe abstraite à l'espace réel où l'œuvre se trouve exhibée et où le spectateur se tient, continuité grâce à quoi celui-ci prend pied là où s'opacifient des figures situées à proximité de lui, qui lui sont présentées comme ses contemporaines et auxquelles il ne peut pas ne pas s'identifier à un certain degré.

Vu, d'une part, que depuis l'avènement de la photographie, qui s'en charge, la peinture est libérée de toute fonction de "reportage" (comme dit Francis

Bacon) de sorte qu'elle n'a plus qu'à développer ses modes propres de figuration, vu également qu'il est impossible, pour le peintre qui traite une figure, de donner par copie le sentiment du réel, car dans ce cas le faux-semblant saute aux yeux, il faut passer par autre chose que la transcription quasi photographique: le spectateur n'aura chance de croire en la figure proposée que si elle porte la marque vivante de la main de l'artiste (faute de quoi le contact ne s'établirait pas) et que s'il y a peu ou prou *distanciation*, distanciation s'il se trouve assez violente pour que des œuvres foncièrement réalistes comme en ont peintes Francis Bacon et son glorieux aîné Picasso prêtent au malentendu consistant à en expliquer la teneur par une visée expressionniste, alors que dans de telles œuvres il n'y a pas accentuation caricaturale relevant de ce que Francis Bacon nomme péjorativement ''illustratif'' mais, ce qui est plus difficile en même temps que plus radical, refonte plastique opérée en profondeur. Procédant à des distorsions non motivées par une intention dramatique voire simplement esthétique, donner d'une réalité vraie ou fictive dont le spectateur, qui la voit projetée sur la toile en grandeur à peu près naturelle, ne doutera pas qu'elle est d'ici et de maintenant une représentation dégagée des perceptions routinières qui font que, dans l'existence courante, on cesse — ou cesserait presque — de voir cette réalité, en offrir une représentation décalée, située hors des habitudes qui éteignent le regard mais renvoyant expressément à notre époque et à notre milieu, n'est-ce pas à cette pratique proche de la transmutation et soumise autant que celle-ci à maints hasards que s'adonne Francis Bacon lorsqu'il peint une figure? En plus d'un cas il y aura donc altération si sévère qu'un fervent d'Oscar Wilde pourrait être porté à croire inconsidérément qu'à l'inverse du fabuleux portrait de Dorian Gray, seul affecté par ce qui ronge son modèle et protégeant l'apparence réelle de celui-ci, les portraits peints par Francis Bacon montrent d'emblée, comme s'ils avaient quelque chose d'oraculaire, leurs modèles en tant que créatures déjà rongées.

Vertu énigmatique, indépendante des esthétiques et rebelle à l'analyse, la présence — contrairement à ce qu'on penserait volontiers — n'est pas une affaire de style: peut en être privée une œuvre très élaborée, exigeant un effort de lecture et requérant une grande activité participante de notre part à nous vague quidam

(comme si cette présence qui constitue la vie même du tableau n'était autre que le présent de la figure en train de se composer dans notre esprit de spectateur à partir des données brutes de la perception), mais peut, inversement, en être douée une œuvre presque naturaliste et qui n'offre, par sa teneur, aucune difficulté de saisie.

Quant aux œuvres de Francis Bacon — du moins celles que, toute question de qualité mise à part, je tiens pour les plus curieusement vivantes — leur intensité extrême me paraît résulter d'une conjugaison paradoxale de ces deux voies: la distorsion plus ou moins poussée des figures coexiste avec un traitement passablement naturaliste des entours. Cause de surprise (vu la distance par rapport à ce qu'on était en droit d'attendre), semblable mariage du chaud et du froid, en éveillant l'attention, ne peut manquer d'accentuer la sensation de présence. Or cette union insolite n'est qu'un exemple entre autres des contradictions que dans sa pratique artistique autant que dans sa vie offre Francis Bacon: en un même tableau coexistence — j'y insiste — de larges secteurs apparemment traités avec indifférence (fonds souvent en aplat) et de morceaux relevant de ce qu'on pourrait appeler la peinture peinturante et qui semblent être le fruit d'un déchaînement de la tête aussi bien que de la main (figures); géométrie relative de l'encadrement dont, généralement, la nette structure contraste avec la forme parfois presque indéfinissable de ces figures qui paraissent éventuellement perdre leur ossature pour se faire étranges glissements ou remous de matière en fusion; dans les portraits essentiellement, libertés qu'autorise le parti pris de ne pas illustrer et contraintes imposées par la volonté d'aboutir à une exacte ressemblance dans la mesure où le permet cette quadrature du cercle, rendre compte de la réaction subjective et quasi arbitraire du peintre à ce qu'il connaît de l'extérieur du personnage sans négliger pour autant les données communes fournies par la photographie, qui en l'occurrence intervient non comme source d'inspiration mais comme moyen de contrôle (sous la forme de photos genre état-civil, aussi peu ''artistes'' que possible et exemptes de tout ce qui serait de nature à soumettre l'imagination à leur dictée, jouant donc en simples garde-fous et non en catalyseurs comme l'ont fait, par exemple, certaines des photos consacrées vers la fin du siècle dernier par Muybridge à l'étude des postures et des mouvements du corps, ou bien des photos médicales montrant des intérieurs de bouches, documents qui maintes fois ont servi à Francis Bacon de points de départ pour son travail); totale laïcité d'un art qui se veut rien que jeu et, réaliste, n'assigne à ses motifs nul autre rôle que d'être ce qu'ils sont, alors que formellement, sans parler des appels directs à la peinture religieuse (telles les *Crucifixions,* qui la plupart n'ont iconographiquement rien à voir avec la mort du Christ mais se développent en triptyques comme pour un cérémonial édifiant dont serait gardée l'ordonnance à défaut du contenu, de même que chez ce quasi-compatriote et quasi-contemporain du peintre, James Joyce, l'ordonnance de l'antique *Odyssée* a servi de modèle à celle du très moderne *Ulysse*), — alors que, dirai-je, cet art à la fois dûment composé et furieusement spontané non seulement procède volontiers d'une convergence modernité et tradition (ainsi le recours fréquent à la forme éminemment classique du triptyque enveloppant en quelque sorte le spectateur, mode dont Francis Bacon m'a dit que c'était en vérité le cinéma sur écran panoramique qui lui avait donné l'idée d'en faire usage) mais, avec le froid cadrage qui si souvent semble vouloir dompter une violence presque sauvage, apparaît empreint d'un ritualisme à tout le moins de surface, comme sur un tout autre plan, celui de la vie courante, l'ordre de la bonne éducation britannique — décorum des rapports privés — est chez Francis Bacon un ordre rien que de courtoisie, fort éloigné d'exclure le désordre et de se transformer en police des désirs.

Distorsion souvent telle qu'elle touche au déchirement, et qui en tout cas donnerait à croire que l'assertion d'André Breton, *la beauté sera convulsive ou ne sera pas,* a été érigée en principe exigeant une absolue obédience; atteinte aux formes naturelles qui peut aller jusqu'au brouillage voire jusqu'à l'effacement; d'une manière ou d'une autre, grave lésion dont le caractère déroutant, gênant et pour certains scandaleux tient au fait que, lorsque Francis Bacon cherche à faire sentir (non à décrire) une réalité donnée ou inventée et que dans ce but il déforme, ce n'est pas seulement à la forme qu'il s'attaque (tels les cubistes, qui eurent tendance à négliger la matérialité des choses pour ne s'en prendre qu'à leurs contours dans leur prodigieuse remise en question des procédés traditionnels d'écriture picturale) mais aussi à la substance du motif, en l'espèce à la chair du modèle qui sera rendue jusque dans sa

chaleur même et dans son élasticité, qualités significatives de vie. Cette façon abrupte qu'a Francis Bacon de s'écarter du motif à seule fin de le retrouver plus parlant représente certes un attentat plus profond, plus réel au réel que si la structure était seule mise en cause: la déformation est d'autant plus fortement reçue comme telle que le motif n'est nullement vidé de sa matérialité, outre qu'il se trouve affirmé expressément actuel (donc voisin de nous) et qu'il y a, en gros, respect relativement naturaliste de la perspective dans le traitement de l'environnement et même du découpé d'ensemble de la figure.

Peintre de personnages qui, dépourvus de toute dimension psychologique, sont toujours pris en tant qu'êtres possédant une substance et recouverts, quand il y a lieu, par une vêture — proposés donc dans leur existence matérielle au sens strict et dans leur existence sociale — Francis Bacon s'avère aussi littéralement matérialiste dans son travail qu'on peut l'attendre de quelqu'un qui notamment, lorsqu'il s'explique sur sa conception de la peinture, se réfère à son ''système nerveux'' plutôt qu'à sa personnalité, montrant ainsi que jusque dans son vocabulaire il ne veut rien idéaliser et qui, par ailleurs, peint sans jamais recourir au dessin proprement dit, comme s'il fuyait l'espèce d'irréalité abstraite de celui-ci et préférait n'user que de couleurs apposées au pinceau ou autrement pour se mettre en quelque sorte en prise directe: refondre non seulement des formes mais, sous les espèces de ces pâtes colorées et autres ingrédients, triturer la matière même, tactique probablement la mieux appropriée pour celui qui, tel Francis Bacon, veut atteindre le tuf, le substrat et, traitant les apparences avec la licence la plus grande, cherche moins à exprimer la chose réelle, soit perçue soit conçue et de toute façon interprétée sur un mode largement subjectif, que — si l'on peut dire — la *réalité de la chose,* son existence même, saisie (s'il se pouvait) par-delà ses caractères circonstanciels et dont en quelque sorte serait retenu le seul mordant, qu'avec ses moyens paradoxaux Francis Bacon parviendrait à faire appréhender de manière aiguë, chance presque égale à celle de qui saurait isoler cette vertu de ''coupage'' ou ''coupaison'' que les lames de rasoir pas encore usées auraient en réserve, si l'on prend au pied de la lettre l'humour pataphysique de Marcel Duchamp.

Décortiquer la chose pour n'en plus garder que la réalité nue, sans doute est-ce cela que Francis Bacon poursuit, la chose en question fût-elle l'un des éléments d'une image générale d'œuvre à faire (base d'un travail tendant à donner corps à cette image qui lui est venue en tête mais au cours duquel, le plus souvent, une tout autre image se substituera à l'originelle), fût-elle cette chose ordinairement réaliste d'esprit mais imaginaire, et non un motif plus ou moins directement emprunté au monde extérieur, ce qui en vérité n'est guère arrivé à Francis Bacon, artiste qui aujourd'hui exécute ses portraits de mémoire, en s'aidant de photographies, et ne fait plus poser, la présence effective du modèle le gênant, dit-il, pour imposer à l'image de celui-ci les déformations voulues (et peut-être, d'une manière générale, parce que le contact avec la réalité vivante à peindre est pour lui chose si poignante qu'il ne saurait l'affronter sans l'intermédiaire de la photographie), déformations qui sont des audaces nécessaires car à défaut l'image ne serait pas plus qu'une effigie, alors qu'avide de présence irrécusable Francis Bacon semble ne pas se contenter d'évoquer des êtres et des choses réels ou imaginaires dont les figures meubleront la surface de sa toile mais tenir, aussi arbitrairement qu'ils puissent être traités, à les faire positivement exister dans l'espace fictif qui leur est alloué. La sensation directe ou par photo interposée primant ici l'idée, et le moteur principal étant le désir véhément de saisir, n'est-ce pas dans un élan de rage autant que d'effusion que Francis Bacon s'en prend à la réalité qu'entre toutes il s'acharne à traduire et ce mouvement éperdu, panique en quelque sorte, ne constitue-t-il pas une rupture affective des limites introduisant dans la texture de la toile ce trouble qu'il ressent, de sorte que c'est moins par distanciation délibérée que par distanciation si l'on peut dire, émotionnelle (souvent poussée au point qu'elle a fait croire que l'artiste figurait volontiers des corps tendant au débordement ou à la liquéfaction) qu'est obtenue cette présence à laquelle pas plus qu'une copie une transcription purement intellectuelle ne permettrait d'atteindre?

''Tentative de capturer l'apparence avec l'ensemble des sensations que cette apparence particulière suscite en moi'', ainsi Francis Bacon définissait-il ce qu'est pour lui le réalisme, dans une lettre qu'il m'adressait et qu'il avait rédigée en français, avec l'aide d'un ami commun, bien qu'en fait il possède admirablement cette langue, mais craint toujours, dans ces discussions serrées dont il paraît avoir le goût, de ne pas la connaître assez pour exprimer sa pensée avec précision et sans possibilité aucune de malentendu. ''Peut-être le réalisme dans son expression la plus profonde, est-il toujours subjectif'', disait-il dans cette même lettre, complément à des conversations que nous avions précédemment eues sur ce sujet qui d'une manière générale me préoccupait et dans l'une desquelles il m'avait fait remarquer qu'il y a aussi des ''réalités intérieures'' et que le réalisme en art ne doit donc pas se confondre avec la simple volonté de traduire en un langage convaincant ce qui existe objectivement.

Que le motif découvert ou imaginé — venu du dehors ou du dedans, prélevé sur la clarté ou arraché à l'ombre — tel que l'a traité ce préparateur ou fabricant, l'artiste, donne au consommateur le sentiment de se trouver devant une réalité neuve qui a plus de poids qu'une image, voilà le sens que me paraît avoir le réalisme de Francis Bacon, un réalisme créateur — comme celui, entre autres, de Picasso — et non seulement transcripteur, un réalisme qui tend moins à figurer qu'à instaurer un réel et qui, parfois, peut même passer thématiquement les bornes de la vraisemblance, sans pour autant se teinter d'idéalité. Cas extrême, dont un bel exemple est fourni par le suffocant tableau de 1982, d'abord triptyque dans le volet central mais finalement unique duquel un corps masculin, solide bloc de chair que supporte une table, dont on voit sur une même ligne les quatre pieds, se résume en un torse sans bras ni tête, sexué cyniquement et sommé d'un double monticule en forme de croupe pulpeuse tournée vers le ciel, cette idole compacte comprenant aussi — outre les pieds chaussés de lourds souliers — deux jambes à demi masquées par des cuissards et des jambières de joueur de hockey qui semblent les paralyser comme feraient des attelles et amener, par une sorte d'antiphrase, à plus franchement les sentir en tant que membres vivants. Suivront, au cours de la même année, un équivalent féminin de ce tableau (le torse acéphale couronné de deux seins, inspiré par un dessin d'Ingres) ainsi qu'un autre torse masculin (somptueusement sculptural mais sans rigidité puisque figuré en mouvement, ce qui n'est pas l'unique tentative, si l'on veut, ''futuriste'' qu'ait faite Francis Bacon de suivre un corps dans son action).

Non ''tranches de vie'' comme chez les écrivains qui se disaient naturalistes, les toiles les plus strictement réalistes mais nullement anecdotiques de Francis Bacon seraient plutôt des sortes de *flashes* comparables à des épiphanies à la Joyce, banalités en coïncidence si parfaite avec leur formulation qu'elles se trouvent soudain promues présences émouvantes, ce que sont: un *Chien* allant vers nous comme à l'aveuglette (1952) ou se promenant flanqué de l'ombre de son maître (*Homme avec un chien,* 1953); fendant de sa vitesse l'air que nous respirons, un garçon cheveux au vent fonçant sur sa bicyclette (*George Dyer à bicyclette,* 1966); une femme debout sur ce trottoir où censément nous sommes, avec à l'arrière-plan une auto circulant sur la chaussée (*Isabel Rawsthorne dans une rue de Soho,* 1967); coiffés de chapeaux mous deux autres Leopold Bloom assis côte à côte comme pour échanger des propos probablement sans intérêt mais qu'il ne tiendrait qu'à nous d'écouter (*Deux figures assises,* 1979).

Bien que le thème d'une toile de Francis Bacon ne soit pas de l'ordre de l'anecdote ou que, du moins, le pouvoir de cette surface peinte au titre jamais raccrocheur ne repose pas essentiellement sur l'événement vrai ou supposé qu'elle évoque — étreinte homosexuelle par exemple ou, comme dans un triptyque de 1971 où l'on reconnaît ce même George Dyer présent dans maints tableaux et qui venait alors de finir tragiquement, homme s'apprêtant à monter un escalier peu éclairé — l'on peut dire qu'une toile de ce genre est avant tout un lieu où il se passe quelque chose, où quelque chose se produit, arrive, en une sorte de *happening* qui n'est somme toute que le surgissement de cette présence à quoi, semble-t-il, tend chacune des œuvres en question et faute de quoi l'activité ouvertement manuelle dont elle résulte resterait nulle et non avenue. Présence qui, le plus souvent, sera présence humaine, mais pourra aussi n'être que présence pour ainsi dire élémentaire d'un fragment de nature dépourvu de tout ce qui pourrait ressembler à une âme: espace herbeux constituant le motif central du *Paysage* de 1978 (pratiquement réduit à un échantillon d'herbage dûment circonscrit pour que, par une espèce d'effet de compression, la transcription ait plus de force), jet d'eau de 1979 (obtenu par effective projection de liquide), tourbillon de sable de 1981 (issu d'un frottis ou d'une pulvérisation), plus récemment — m'a confié l'intéressé — eau coulant d'un robinet. Présence que, dans le cas de cette présence humaine qui semble être pour Francis Bacon à travers ses différentes périodes l'objectif majeur jamais atteint avec assez d'évidence, divers moyens éloignés de tout expressionnisme paraissent quelquefois viser obliquement à intensifier, ce qu'attestent plus d'une œuvre de Francis Bacon (toiles ou triptyques) des années 60 et 70: ombre portée prenant la forme éminemment matérielle d'une flaque que sécréterait la figure dotée ainsi d'un plus grand poids; reflet comme un appendice ou un double de même densité que l'original confirmé dans sa réalité par cette répétition; élision d'une partie du corps considéré ou inversement accent mis sur elle par un ajout (figuration vériste d'attelles ou autres accessoires destinés à pallier un dommage physique mais qui, en vérité, soulignent plutôt qu'ils ne cachent) ou, parfois aussi, position problématique si ce n'est acrobatique de ce corps apparemment menacé dans son équilibre sinon au bord de la chute et, dirait-on, se trouvant de ce fait plus conscient de lui-même et, partant, s'avérant plus éloquent pour le tiers qui regarde; voire, à l'occasion, geste qui frappera d'autant plus qu'on le verra accompli par un organe autre que le préposé (ainsi l'homme tournant une clef dans une serrure avec son pied, thème principal d'une *Peinture,* 1978). Par des voies souvent des plus détournées, c'est une quête de réalité aussitôt perceptible — ou, plus précisément, de résonance concrète donnant d'emblée au spectateur l'impression de prendre langue avec le réel — que Francis Bacon semble mener dans son travail, toujours tendu à l'extrême car c'est par le jeu actif de forces contraires, volonté réaliste et désir de transcrire avec une liberté totale, soit par plus qu'une opposition romantique et purement extérieure de contrastes, qu'un artiste a le plus de chances d'atteindre ce but: faire qu'une présence confondante se manifeste dans toute sa ''brutalité de fait'' (selon les termes de l'interlocuteur de David Sylvester) et subjugue par la vie particulière que le regard lui prête.

Or, pour qu'à nos yeux la figure à deux dimensions inscrite sur la toile soit douée d'une vie captivante encore que nous la sachions factice (étrangère à la biologie et procédant de l'ingéniosité humaine), suffit-il que cette figure apparaisse non comme la copie inerte d'une réalité mais comme le produit original de la reprise de celle-ci par une imagination et qu'elle nous parle de quelque chose de tout proche dans l'espace et dans le temps? Qu'il ait été conscient ou non d'une telle insuffisance, le fait est que Francis Bacon, spontanément sans doute et moins après calcul que dans la chaleur de l'action, ne s'est pas privé, tant s'en faut, de faire intervenir l'irrationnel dans la confection et dans l'agencement de ses toiles, ce qui dans la mesure même où la logique est ainsi bousculée leur infuse un surcroît de vie. Non seulement il a toujours beaucoup compté sur ce que dans ses conversations avec David Sylvester il appelle l' ''accident'' (bavure du pinceau ou de la brosse, lapsus manuel ou tout autre écart involontaire altérant ce qu'on entendait faire) et il n'a pas laissé non plus de spéculer sur l'appel délibéré au hasard (projections directes de couleurs ou frottages au chiffon dont les résultats aléatoires avaient du moins l'avantage d'éloigner de l' ''illustration'' l'œuvre ainsi agressée, voire de permettre de prendre un nouveau départ), mais on voit souvent intégré à un tableau de lui tel ou tel détail apparemment gratuit, qui semble n'avoir aucune justification thématique et dont on peut penser que, même s'il était appelé par une exigence picturale, celle-ci était du moins assez lâche pour que l'artiste y répondît d'une façon résolument arbitraire, de sorte que la toile ainsi soustraite aux normes idéales se trouve porter ouvertement la marque de cette contingence inhérente à tout ce qui, sur notre globe, est venu à la vie. Cercle plein ou tracé circulaire, ellipse ou bien tache sans forme définie, posés ici ou là — sans rime ni raison, dirait-on —, flèche indicatrice qui non seulement accroche mais paraît vouloir orienter le regard, ou encore longue traînée de peinture blanche évoquant une brusque coulée ou un coup de fouet, de tels accents attisent dans la mesure même où, dénués de sens ou purement signalisateurs, ils constituent à quelque degré des éléments de caprice ou de désordre (libertés prises ou transgression) par rapport à l'ordre relatif de l'ensemble signifiant qui, si une certaine dose de folie ne s'y mêlait, serait une composition plus ou moins intéressante ou agréable, voire passionnante, mais non cette chose vibrante de vie que, dans son incertitude foncière, il est.

Aviver la — ou les — figure, ponctuer à sa guise ce que l'on montre, plutôt que se plier à des impératifs organiques de construction (ce qui serait tendre au décoratif), voilà selon moi l'une des règles d'or que, d'instinct peut-on présumer, applique Francis Bacon. Cela

expliquerait pourquoi, par exemple, il lui est arrivé d'engager entièrement ou presque telle figure — plutôt refondue, voire bouleversée, que littéralement restructurée — dans une sorte de cadre plus restreint s'ajoutant à celui, général, du tableau: un bâti géométrique nullement représentatif mais seulement linéaire et qui, en même temps qu'il joue comme un terme moyen entre la figure et le cadre réel et n'est pas sans évoquer la portion d'espace dans laquelle le personnage est censé se tenir, semble constituer une cage, aux arêtes seules visibles, où la figure serait plus ou moins encaquée comme si, pour porter sa force à un maximum, il fallait enclore, sertir, enchâsser, ce morceau librement et fougueusement peint que, dans le même but d'exaltation au sens strict, Francis Bacon fera voir quelquefois aussi se détachant sur un écran, autre mode simple et efficace de mise en évidence.

Soit en situant nettement grâce à un simulacre d'armature géométrique, soit en pourvoyant d'un fond qui joue le rôle de repoussoir, il semble que Francis Bacon s'emploie souvent tantôt à isoler pour que cela ressorte mieux, tantôt à faire se détacher certaines parties du tableau qu'il n'hésite pas à promouvoir au rang de vedettes: celles qui grâce à leur thème apparaîtront comme les plus vivantes et par rapport auxquelles le reste ne sera que dispositif scénique, lieu aménagé pour que la chose s'y passe. Sans doute est-ce dans le même esprit qu'il surhausse volontiers ses figures, soit au moyen d'un socle d'ailleurs peu élevé supportant le meuble sur lequel le personnage en question est assis ou couché, soit en les séparant franchement du sol (comme dans le triptyque de 1970 où trois figures féminines sont présentées juchées sur une espèce de longue poutre incurvée traversant l'ensemble tripartite, ou cet autre de la même année dans chaque volet latéral duquel un homme est montré assis sur un siège apparemment équipé d'agrès comme pourrait l'être un siège de balançoire). Il faut noter, du reste, que dans ses propos Francis Bacon — constatant ce fait sans chercher à en démêler les causes, que l'on peut présumer situées à un niveau des plus déterminants en même temps que des plus lointains — ne cache pas l'intérêt particulier qu'a pour lui le surhaussement, du moins (convient-il d'ajouter) quand c'est une personne humaine qui en est l'objet. Ne déclare-t-il pas, par exemple, avoir été très impressionné — sous l'angle impie du spectacle — par une photo où l'on voit le pape porté à bras et épaules d'hommes sur la *sedia gestatoria* utilisée lors de son intronisation ou bien ne dit-il pas retenir essentiellement du thème de la crucifixion, non le drame religieux dont le divin supplicié est le protagoniste, mais — outre l'aspect boucherie revêtu objectivement par l'événement — la situation spatiale du Christ en croix, qui se trouve précisément surhaussé? Assurément l'art de Francis Bacon, matérialisé par des créations étrangères à toute croyance et dont il affirme qu'elles ne sont porteuses d'aucun message, s'avère d'une laïcité, d'une positivité trop grandes pour que parler de *sacré* à ce sujet ne soit pas téméraire. Il n'en est pas moins vrai que cet art qu'en principe il tient pour rien de plus qu'un jeu, comme tout art de nos jours, et dont, loin de feindre d'oublier qu'il en tire de substantiels profits, il le rappelle avec humour (façon de rabaisser qui en quelque mesure procède du nihilisme dada et de la remise en cause non seulement des esthétiques traditionnelles mais du bien-fondé de l'art même et donc de l'attitude "artiste"), ne laisse pas d'aboutir fréquemment à des œuvres qu'on peut sans aberration regarder comme dotées d'une aura de sacré, non certes en raison de leur contenu, puisqu'il s'agit — il importe d'y insister — d'un art profondément réaliste, d'un art sans allusions, tel que ce qui est donné est donné sans qu'il y ait rien à voir derrière la représentation proposée, mais parce que chacune des œuvres en question paraît relever d'un protocole privilégiant certains éléments qui sembleront d'autant plus vivants qu'on les aura visiblement soustraits à la platitude du profane (mis hors du commun, arrachés au quotidien, placés sur le podium au propre ou au figuré, par divers artifices soulignant ce qu'a fait la peinture là où la fureur de peindre s'est, comme par chance, déchaînée). Par des moyens de plusieurs sortes, isolement des figures comme si, malgré leur prosaïsme, elles étaient d'intouchables idoles; ambiguïté de ces figures nullement expressionnistes mais souvent distordues au point d'être, en fait, propres à déclencher un sentiment proche de ce mélange d'extase et d'angoisse qu'on nomme horreur sacrée et qui est peut-être éprouvé avec le plus d'acuité quand, moment vertigineux aux sources variables à l'extrême, il semble que l'on entre en contact intime avec la réalité enfin mise à nu; quant à plusieurs de ces figures, brouillage partiel qui semble les marquer délibérément de secret sans effacer en rien leur caractère réaliste; en dehors de toute visée au sublime et plus percutante de ce fait, solennité de l'agencement général, spécialement dans les triptyques; fréquemment, comme dans les tableaux de siècles révolus où sont pieusement figurés les donateurs, intervention d'assesseurs et parfois d'assesseurs au second degré (assesseurs d'assesseurs pourrait-on croire) qui semblent avoir, tels des officiants ou servants, leur place hiérarchiquement assignée dans un cérémonial et jouer le rôle d'une sorte de garde d'honneur par rapport à la figure principale, ainsi dotée d'un prestige ou pouvoir plus grand tout comme, aux mêmes fins d'intensification de la présence de pareilles figures, il arrive également que Francis Bacon emploie comme faire-valoir des manières de tableaux dans le tableau, en l'espèce portraits masculins en buste qui ne sont manifestement que portraits... Est-il abusif de considérer que ces traits ont les uns comme les autres pour effet de conférer cette capacité précise aux œuvres ainsi conçues: prendre le spectateur aux rets d'une liturgie en quelque sorte *à blanc* qui, sans référence à quelque transcendance que ce soit et n'existant que pour elle-même, l'émeut d'autant plus puissamment que ne l'embrume aucun sous-entendu?

Réaliste puisque, même quand il ne ferme pas la porte à l'invraisemblable, sa visée dernière semble être d'exprimer la vie (celle que nous vivons, ce que nous sentons, l'être mouvant que nous sommes) et de produire une œuvre douée de cette présence qui est le rayonnement de sa vie à elle, perçue sans qu'aucune distance mentale interpose son brouillard, — réaliste authentique mais hostile à l'anecdote qui, même sérieuse, ne touche qu'à une écume de la réalité, Francis Bacon s'est gardé d'encombrer ses toiles de quoi que ce soit de dramatique au sens strict, en d'autres termes d'y faire jouer le ressort d'une intrigue dont la saisie par l'intellect serait un détour amoindrissant l'impact sensoriel de l'œuvre, et a usé tout au plus de scénarios réduits à presque rien (le plus loquace étant sans doute celui du volet central de la *Crucifixion* 1965, où un homme dont on ne voit guère que la cocarde tricolore est molesté par le porteur d'un brassard à croix gammée, détail dont l'auteur nie d'ailleurs la signification historique, le justifiant simplement par le besoin où il était d'une tache de couleur en cet endroit et par le fait que l'idée de ce brassard provenait d'une vieille photo journalistique montrant Hitler entouré d'autres nazis). Reste pourtant que, trop épris de la vie pour en rejeter fût-ce la contre-partie mortelle qu'implique son défaut de fixité, il s'est ouvert plusieurs fois, assurément pas au drame — trop proche du fait divers et devant par trop au récit — mais à la tragédie qui, sans rien éveiller de sentimental, touche en lui le sensitif frappé par l'''odeur de mort'' qu'il prête aux lieux où sont exposées des viandes de boucherie. Non seulement les diverses *Crucifixions,* d'où l'événement narré par les Evangiles fut vite évacué totalement, restent marquées d'un sceau de sang (chairs mises à mal) et un triptyque très ancien (*Trois études pour des figures à la base d'une Crucifixion,* 1944) est fondé quant à lui sur un thème emprunté à l'une des branches les plus noires de la mythologie des Grecs, la vindicte exercée par les Erinyes, mais un autre beaucoup plus récent (1981) a été expressément inspiré par *L'Orestie* d'Eschyle. Or on constate que si cette composition est indubitablement empreinte d'un caractère tragique, c'est en l'absence de tout pathos et sans qu'elle contienne aucun élément tant soit peu théâtral: dans cette œuvre simple et directe jouent seules la fermeté de la structure d'ensemble et la consistance marmoréenne des figures présentées, qualités conformes à la nature même de la tragédie qui, à l'inverse du drame où les gens agissent mus par leurs sentiments et au gré des circonstances, fait de ses personnages bâtis d'un bloc les jouets de dures obligations ou de fatalités. Ici encore, c'est sans passer par la moindre anecdote que Francis Bacon manifeste son esprit profondément réaliste même quand il se tourne vers le mythe: ce qu'il nous montre ne fait rien qu'être là, épiphanique, et de texture trop dense pour que nous puissions le récuser. De même, le triptyque de 1976, donc antérieur à celui-ci de quelques années, triptyque centré sur la figure — que je dirai volontiers prométhéenne — d'un homme à la tête fouaillée et réduite à rien par le bec d'un rapace aux ailes déployées, volatile de même famille que celui qu'on verra, plus modeste, au pied d'une bête écorchée (un porc, semble-t-il) dans le tableau de 1980 intitulé *Carcasse de viande et oiseau de proie,* œuvre qui elle non plus ne saurait fournir la matière d'un discours voire d'un argument tant soit peu détaillé mais atteint au tragique d'une scène sacrificielle par la majesté de sa structure et celle de la couleur de la pièce de boucherie haut suspendue. Faut-il enfin noter qu'en 1969, lorsqu'il a peint ses trois *Corridas* d'une vérité d'autant

plus étonnante qu'elles viennent de quelqu'un qui n'est pas un aficionado, Francis Bacon s'est attaqué, dans un esprit réaliste, à ce qui apparaît à nombre d'entre nous comme l'un des avatars modernes de l'antique tragédie.

Sous le verre qui, selon lui, est un moyen d' ''aplanir'' leurs inégalités matérielles de facture, mais dont je me demande pourtant si son rôle ne serait pas aussi de tempérer un peu la virulence réaliste de ces œuvres, voire de donner quelque apparat à ces présentations de personnages généralement surpris, dirait-on, soit dans la chaude mêlée du commerce érotique, soit dans les postures les plus banales de la veille ou du sommeil quand ce n'est les plus bassement fonctionnelles, d'étendre par ailleurs à la totalité du tableau (y compris le décor sans relief) et de parfaire, grâce à un englobement presque littéral, le travail de mise à part, de soustraction à la neutralité quotidienne, qui pour certains de ses éléments s'est effectué selon des voies diverses, les toiles à la fois si effervescentes et si contrôlées de Francis Bacon offrent à qui, d'un coup d'œil d'ensemble, en embrasse la diversité une frappante image de ce qu'est ce contemporain singulier dans toute la complexité que j'espérais notablement réduire en le considérant dans le miroir de son art. Espoir à peu près vain: faire le portrait de l'art de Francis Bacon, aussi enseignants que soient les entretiens de cet artiste avec son ami David Sylvester, se révèle en fin de compte presque aussi difficultueux que le portraiturer lui-même, et guère plus éclairant (plus simplificateur). L'échec serait donc indéniable si, après ce rapide survol qui ne prétendait nullement détecter des dessous symboliques là où il n'y a pas à en chercher, il n'était malgré tout possible d'indiquer ce que, d'une manière très générale, un tel art nous donne à entendre.

Bien que leur auteur affirme qu'il ne délivre aucun message, je constate par expérience personnelle que pareilles œuvres aident puissamment à sentir ce que pour un homme sans illusions est le fait d'exister, sensation qui en l'occurrence sera d'autant plus aiguë que c'est dans un présent clairement explicité par maints détails qu'ici la peinture fait bel et bien acte de présence, pour elle-même et comme créatrice d'images qui, en ces œuvres *actuelles* autant par l'action qu'elles exercent sur nous que par leur actualité chronologique, n'ont d'autre raison d'être qu'une présence presque blessante. De plus, ne semble-t-il pas qu'un art de cette espèce, où presque dans chaque image la beauté et sa négation apparaissent souverainement conjuguées, fasse écho à la double nature des moments que nous goûtons comme nos moments peut-être les plus spécifiquement humains, ceux dans lesquels — fascinés, séduits jusqu'au vertige — nous croyons toucher à la réalité même, vivre enfin notre vie, mais constatons qu'à notre joie s'associe une étrange dissonance: l'angoisse que suscite cette instance radicalement ennemie, la mort, que toute saisie apparemment plénière de la vie nous dénonce siégeant au plus intime de nous? Ambivalence fondamentale, qui est peut-être ce qui porte essentiellement Francis Bacon, artiste hypersensible et férocement avide de réalité, à traiter comme d'autres pourraient le faire d'une chose sacrée la réalité qu'il instaure en peignant: par des voies diverses, la mettre entre guillemets ou en exergue, comme une merveille que son caractère équivoque (mi-ensorcellement mi-menace) appellerait à juguler autant qu'à l'exalter.

A propos de ces toiles dont la modernité plonge ses racines au plus profond et n'est pas réductible à un piquant de simple surface, David Sylvester parle de "pertinence", leur attribuant cette vertu qui consiste à tomber pile, faire ou dire quand il le faut ce qu'il faut faire ou dire. Exemptes de double fond et n'ayant pas à être lues au-delà de ce qui est vu, puisque l'auteur se défend de vouloir, en peignant, dire plus que ce qu'il peint et coupe donc court à tout commentaire idéologique, ces tableaux qui, lieux de pures présences vivantes ne débouchant sur rien, sont placés sous le signe de l'absence de sens — autrement dit *non-sens* — semblent, dans leur éclatante nudité de l'instant même (dénuée d'en-deçà comme d'au-delà et empêtrée par rien qui de près ou de loin tienne à la littérature), des images en accord avec l'inanité de notre situation au sein de ce monde dont, éphémères, nous ne sommes que des éléments capables entre tous d'ivresses brillantes et inutiles. Réponses somme toute à l'état d'esprit qui est sans doute ce que naguère on eût dit notre mal du siècle: conscience ardente d'être présence ouverte à tous les attraits d'un monde au demeurant peu prodigue

en douceur, mais glaciale certitude de n'être que cela, sans vrai pouvoir, et de l'être seulement pour un temps ridiculement mesuré.

A l'instar d'un Samuel Beckett dont les phrases sans mystère apparent font songer aux exhalaisons discrètes d'un feu de tourbe, Francis Bacon exprime — sans inflation rhétorique ni détour mythologique, sous des aspects aptes à nous combler par la justesse et la vigueur de la formule, alors que devrait nous accabler la dure vérité qui trouve ici à tacitement se formuler — ce qu'est au vrai notre condition propre (expressément celle du dépossédé de tout paradis durable qu'est l'homme d'aujourd'hui qui, yeux ouverts, sait se pencher sur lui-même) et l'on est, à ce titre, fondé à l'étiqueter réaliste, aussi fort que soit — à un niveau moins journalier — la composante tragique, pointant assurément ici et là, mais explicitement manifestée tant par le triptyque en rapport avec *L'Orestie* que par la référence aux Erinyes (soit brutale comme dans les *Trois études pour des figures à la base d'une Crucifixion,* soit par ricochet comme dans la libre paraphrase plastique de *Sweeney agonistes,* poème dont l'une des épigraphes, tirée des *Choéphores,* fait entendre Oreste parlant de ses persécutrices). Si le gain le plus solide obtenu par un tel artiste à travers son propos direct de représentation, est de rendre sensible aux spectateurs immédiatement fascinés la bizarrerie, si ce n'est l'absurdité, de leur existence même (contingence sans réponse et tout au plus questionnante), cet artiste ne peut — en dehors même de toute visée au pathétique — que leur en montrer le revers atroce conjoint à un avers scintillant. Expression authentique d'un Occidental de notre temps, le travail de Francis Bacon — homme qui lui-même s'est admirablement expliqué sur ce qu'il est et sur ce qu'il nous apporte en parlant de ce qu'il nomme nietzschéennement son "désespoir joyeux" (*exhilarating despair*) — ne peut pas ne refléter en rien, si résolu qu'il soit à ne pas faire une peinture tant soit peu discoureuse, le trouble lancinant de quiconque vit dans ce temps d'horreur saupoudré de merveille et le regarde lucidement.

*Michel Leiris*

# CHRONOLOGY

**1909**

Born in Dublin, 28 October, of English parents, the second of five children. Father a breeder and trainer of racehorses. He is a collateral descendant of the famous Elizabethan philosopher, Francis Bacon.

**1914**

At the outbreak of war, the family moves to London and his father joins the War Office. Thereafter they move back and forth between England and Ireland changing houses every year or two — never having a permanent home.

**1925**

Bacon suffers from asthma as a child and is privately tutored — never has any schooling in the conventional sense. Leaves home at the age of 16 to go to London. Works for a short time as a servant to a solicitor and later in an office for several months.

**1927-28**

Travels to Berlin, stays for two months only, then on to Paris where he occasionally secures commissions for interior decoration. Visits a Picasso exhibition at the Paul Rosenberg Gallery which greatly impresses him and inspires him to start making drawings and watercolours.

**1929**

Returns to London. Exhibits in his Queensbury Mews studio furniture and rugs made from his own designs. Begins painting in oils (self-taught).

**1930**

Arranges a joint exhibition in his studio with Roy de Maistre, showing furniture as well as paintings and gouaches. *The Studio* magazine features a double page article on his studio titled ''The 1930 Look in British Decoration''.

**1931**

Moves to the Fulham Road. Gradually abandons his work as a decorator in order to devote himself to painting. Earns his living by doing odd jobs, none of them connected with art.

**1933**

Paints *Crucifixion 1933* which is reproduced in Herbert Read's *Art Now*.

**1934**

Stages his first one-man show at the Transition Gallery, Sunderland House. Discouraged at its lack of success, he paints less and less and starts to gamble.

**1936**

Submits some work to the International Surrealist Exhibition. It is rejected as ''not sufficiently surreal''.

**1937**

Takes part in an important group exhibition ''Young British Painters'' at Agnews, London, organized by his friend Eric Hall. Other artists include Roy de Maistre, Graham Sutherland, Victor Pasmore and Ivon Hitchens.

**1941-44**

Moves for a short time to a cottage in Petersfield, Hampshire. Returns to London and rents Millais's old studio in Kensington. Destroys nearly all his earlier works (only ten canvases remain from the period 1929-44). Declared unfit for military service because of his asthma and is assigned to Civil Defence (ARP).

**1944-45**

Resumes painting in earnest and executes the triptych *Three Studies for Figures at the Base of a Crucifixion* which causes considerable consternation when shown at the Lefevre Gallery in April 1945. The mysterious forms were regarded as freaks, monsters irrelevant to the concerns of the day, and the product of an imagination so eccentric as not to count in any permanent way. The triptych is acquired by the Tate Gallery in 1953.

**1945-46**

Exhibits *Figure in a Landscape* and *Figure Study II* in group exhibitions held at the Lefevre and Redfern Galleries. Other artists include Matthew Smith, Henry Moore and Graham Sutherland.

**1946-50**

Lives mainly in Monte Carlo. Friendship with Graham Sutherland.

**1948**

Alfred H. Barr purchases *Painting 1946*, one of his most important works, for the Museum of Modern Art, New York.

**1949**

One-man show at the Hanover Gallery, London, who become his agent for the next ten years. Begins painting the series of Heads (including *Head VI*, which is regarded as the first of the ''Pope'' paintings and *Head IV (Man with Monkey)*. Uses Eadweard Muybridge's photographic studies *Animal Locomotion* and *Human Figure in Motion* as a source of reference for his paintings of animals and the human figure.

**1950**

Teaches briefly at the Royal College of Art as deputy for John Minton. Travels to South Africa to visit his mother; spends a few days in Cairo.

**1951-55**

Changes studios several times. For a short time (1953) shares a house with David Sylvester.

**1951**

First portrait of Lucian Freud.

**1952**

Exhibits landscapes inspired by Africa and the South of France.

**1953**

First one-man show outside Britain at Durlacher Brothers, New York. Paints *Two Figures* (The Wrestlers), considered by many as one of his greatest paintings.

## 1954

Paints the *Man in Blue* series. Together with Ben Nicholson and Lucian Freud, represents Great Britain at the XXVII Venice Biennale. Takes opportunity to visit Ostia and Rome but does not attend the Biennale nor see the Velázquez portrait of *Pope Innocent X*, the reproduction of which inspired his series of "Popes".

## 1955

First retrospective exhibition at the Institute of Contemporary Arts, London. Paints portraits of the collectors Robert and Lisa Sainsbury who become his patrons.

## 1956

Visits Tangier to see his friend Peter Lacey. Rents a flat and returns there frequently during the next three years.

## 1957

First exhibition in Paris at the Galerie Rive Droite. Exhibits the Van Gogh Series at the Hanover Gallery, London.

## 1958

First one-man exhibitions in Italy; shows in Turin, Milan and Rome. Signs contract with Marlborough Fine Art Ltd. London.

## 1959

Exhibition at the V São Paulo Biennale.
Paints for a while in St. Ives, Cornwall.

## 1960

First exhibition at Marlborough Fine Art, London.

## 1962

Paints his first large triptych *Three Studies for a Crucifixion* acquired by the Solomon R. Guggenheim Museum, New York. Major retrospective exhibition at the Tate Gallery, London. Modified version shown in Mannheim, Turin and Zurich (1963). Death of Peter Lacey.

## 1963

Paints *Landscape near Malabata* in memory of Peter Lacey.

## 1963-64

Retrospective exhibition at the Solomon R. Guggenheim Museum, New York, and afterwards at the Art Institute of Chicago.

## 1964

Friendship with George Dyer who becomes a model for many of his paintings. Executes large Triptych *3 figures in a room* acquired by the Musée National d'Art Moderne, Paris.
Paints *Double Portrait of Lucian Freud and Frank Auerbach* acquired by Moderna Museet, Stockholm.

## 1965

Paints large *Crucifixion* Triptych acquired by Munich Museum.

## 1966

Exhibits at the Galerie Maeght, Paris. The artist attends the Opening. The exhibition travels to Marlborough Fine Art, London (1967).

## 1967

Awarded the Painting Prize at the 1967 Pittsburgh International and the Rubens Prize by the City of Siegen.

## 1968

Short visit to New York for exhibition of his recent paintings at the Marlborough-Gerson Gallery.

## 1971-72

Important retrospective exhibition at the Grand Palais, Paris; subsequently shown at the Kunsthalle, Dusseldorf.
Death in Paris of his friend and model George Dyer (1971). Paints large *Triptych 1971* in his memory.

## 1972-74

Executes series of three large Triptychs (sometimes known as the *Black triptychs - 1972, 1973, 1974*) influenced by the death of George Dyer.

## 1975

Major exhibition *Recent Painting 1968-74* selected by Henry Geldzahler at the Metropolitan Museum of Art, New York. Travels to New York to attend Opening and stays ten days.

## 1977

Galerie Claude Bernard, Paris, organizes an important exhibition of recent work. *Le tout Paris* attends the Private View at which the Artist is present. The Gallery is full to overflowing (7,000 visitors); crowds block the streets and the police are forced to close adjoining roads.

## 1978

Brief visit to Rome to meet Balthus at the Villa Medici.

## 1980

One-man show of recent work at the Marlborough Gallery Inc., New York.

## 1983

Francis Bacon lives and works in London — with occasional visits to France.


## ONE-MAN EXHIBITIONS

## 1934

Transition Gallery, London.

## 1949

Hanover Gallery, London.

## 1950

Hanover Gallery, London.

## 1951-52

Hanover Gallery, London.

## 1952-53

Hanover Gallery, London.

**1953**
Durlacher Brothers, New York.
Beaux-Arts Gallery, London.

**1954**
Hanover Gallery, London.

**1955**
Institute of Contemporary Arts, London.

**1957**
Galerie Rive Droite, Paris.

**1958**
Galleria Galatea, Turin, afterwards at the Galleria dell'Ariete, Milan and l'Obelisco, Rome.

**1959**
Richard Feigen Gallery, Chicago.
Hanover Gallery, London.

**1960**
Marlborough Fine Art, London.

**1961**
Nottingham University, Nottingham.

**1962**
Retrospective Exhibition, Tate Gallery, London. Modified version toured the Kunsthalle, Mannheim; Galleria Civica d'Arte Moderna, Turin; Kunsthaus, Zurich; and (in 1963) the Stedelijk Museum, Amsterdam.

**1962**
Galleria d'Arte Galatea, Milan.

**1963**
Marlborough Fine Art, London.
Granville Gallery, New York.

**1963-64**
Solomon R. Guggenheim Museum, New York and afterwards at the Art Institute of Chicago.

**1964**
Contemporary Arts Association, Houston, Texas.

**1965**
Retrospective Exhibition, Kunstverein, Hamburg, afterwards at Moderna Museet, Stockholm and the Municipal Gallery of Modern Art, Dublin.
Marlborough Fine Art, London.

**1966**
Galleria Toninelli, Milan.
Galerie Maeght, Paris.

**1967**
Marlborough Galleria d'Arte, Rome.
Galleria Toninelli, Milan.
Marlborough Fine Art, London.
Oberes Schloss, Siegen (Rubens Prize Exhibition).

**1968**
Marlborough-Gerson Gallery, New York.

**1970**
Galleria d'Arte Galatea, Turin.

**1971-72**
Retrospective Exhibition, Grand Palais, Paris and afterwards at Kunsthalle, Düsseldorf.

**1975**
Recent Paintings 1968-74, Metropolitan Museum of Art, New York.
Marlborough Galerie, Zurich.

**1976**
Musée Cantini, Marseilles.

**1977**
Galerie Claude Bernard, Paris.

**1977-78**
Museo de Arte Moderno, Mexico and afterwards at Museo de Arte Contemporáneo, Caracas.

**1978**
Fundación Juan March, Madrid and afterwards at Fundació Joan Miró, Barcelona.

**1980**
Marlborough Gallery Inc., New York.

**1983**
National Museum of Modern Art, Tokyo; National Museum, Kyoto; Aichi Prefectural Art Gallery, Nagoya.

# BIBLIOGRAPHY

## MONOGRAPHS

### 1964

Rothenstein, Sir John, and Alley, Ronald, *Francis Bacon,* Catalogue Raisonné, Thames and Hudson, London. 292 pp. illus.

Russell, John, *Francis Bacon,* Series "Art in Progress", Methuen & Co., London. 26 pp. illus.

### 1963-67

Rothenstein, Sir John, *Francis Bacon,* The Masters, Fratelli Fabbri, Milan 1963; Purnell and Sons. Ltd., London, No. 71, 244 pp. illus.; Hachette, Paris, 1967, 12 pp. illus.

### 1971

Russell, John, *Francis Bacon,* Thames and Hudson, London; Les Editions du Chêne, Paris; Propylaen Verlag, Berlin. 242 pp. illus.

### 1974

Leiris, Michel, *Francis Bacon ou la Vérité criante,* Éditions Fata Morgana, Paris.

### 1975

Sylvester, David, *Interviews with Francis Bacon,* Thames and Hudson, London and Pantheon Books Inc., New York, 128 pp. illus.; *L'Art de l'impossible* (French edition of Interviews by David Sylvester). Preface by Michel Leiris, Series "Les Sentiers de la Creation" Editions Albert Skira, Geneva 1976; *Entrevistas con Francis Bacon* (Spanish edition), Ediciones Polígrafa, S.A., Barcelona, 1977; *Samtal med Francis Bacon* (Swedish edition), Forum Stockholm 1977. New enlarged edition published by Thames and Hudson, London, 1980. *Gespräche mit Francis Bacon* (German edition), Prestel Verlag, Munich, 1982.

Trucchi, Lorenza, *Francis Bacon,* Fratelli Fabbri Editori, Milan, 1975; English Edition, Thames and Hudson, London, and Abrams, New York, 1976.

### 1978

*Bacon* Opus International No. 68, Editions George Fall, Paris.

### 1979

Russell, John, *Francis Bacon* (revised edition), World of Art Series, Thames and Hudson, London, Oxford University Press, New York, 192 pp. illus.

### 1981

Deleuze, Gilles, *Francis Bacon, Logique de la Sensation,* Editions de la Différence, Paris, 2 vols. 112 pp. and 164 pp. illus.

## FILMS

### 1962-63

*Francis Bacon: Paintings 1944-62,* conceived and directed by David Thompson, music by Elizabeth Lutyens. Film made for the Arts Council of Great Britain and Marlborough Fine Art Ltd., by Samaritan Films, London. Distributed by Gala Films.

### 1966

*Sunday Night Francis Bacon. Interviews with David Sylvester,* directed by Michael Gill for BBC Television, London. Extracts reproduced in catalogue *Bacon* exhibition, Marlborough Fine Art Ltd., London, 1967.

### 1971

*Francis Bacon.* Interview with Maurice Chapuis, directed by J. M. Berzosa for ORTF Television, Paris. Film made in connection with Bacon retrospective exhibition at the Grand Palais, Paris, 1971.

*Review - Francis Bacon,* produced by Colin Nears, directed by Gavin Millar, for BBC Television, London. Film made in connection with the Bacon retrospective exhibition at the Grand Palais, Paris, 1971.

### 1974

*Portrait of Francis Bacon,* directed by Thomas Ayck for NDR Television, Hamburg.

### 1975

*Interviews with Bacon by David Sylvester,* Aquarius, London Weekend Television.

# PUBLIC COLLECTIONS

**AUSTRALIA**
Adelaide — National Gallery of South Australia
Canberra — National Gallery of Australia
Melbourne — The National Gallery of Victoria
Sydney — Art Gallery of New South Wales

**BELGIUM**
Brussels — Musées Royaux des Beaux-Arts de Belgique
Ghent — Musée des Beaux-Arts
Liège — Musée des Beaux-Arts

**CANADA**
Ottawa — The National Gallery of Canada

**FINLAND**
Helsinki — Art Museum Atheneum

**FRANCE**
Marseille — Musée Cantini
Paris — Musée National d'Art Moderne, Centre Georges Pompidou

**GERMANY**
Berlin — Nationalgalerie
Bochum — Städtische Kunstgalerie
Cologne — Wallraf-Richartz Museum, Ludwig Collection
Düsseldorf — Kunstsammlung Nordrhein-Westfalen
Frankfurt — Städelches Kunstinstitut
Hamburg — Kunsthalle
Hanover — Kunstmuseum
Mannheim — Kunsthalle
Munich — Staatsgalerie Modern Kunst
Stuttgart — Staatsgalerie
Wuppertal — Von der Heydt Museum

**GREAT BRITAIN & N. IRELAND**
Aberdeen — Art Gallery
Belfast — Ulster Museum
Birmingham — City Art Gallery
Cardiff — National Museum of Wales
Huddersfield — Art Gallery, Kirklees Metropolitan Council
Leeds — Temple Newsam House
Leicester — Museum and Art Gallery
London — The Arts Council of Great Britain
Royal College of Art
The Tate Gallery
Manchester — City Art Gallery
Whitworth Art Gallery
Newcastle-upon-Tyne — King's College Hatton Gallery
Norwich — University of East Anglia
Oxford — Pembroke College

**ISRAEL**
Jerusalem — Bezalel National Museum

**ITALY**
Milan — Brera Museum of Modern Art
Rome — Vatican Museum of Modern Art
Turin — Galleria Civica d'Arte Moderna

**JAPAN**
Fukuoka — Museum of Art
Toyama — Museum of Modern Art

**MEXICO**
Mexico City — Museo Rufino Tamayo

**NETHERLANDS**
Amsterdam — Stedelijk Museum
Eindhoven — Stedelijk Van Abbemuseum
The Hague — Gemeentemuseum
Rotterdam — Boymans Van Beuningen Museum

**SPAIN**
Bilbao — Museo de Bellas Artes

**SWEDEN**
Gothenburg — Art Gallery
Stockholm — Moderna Museet

**SWITZERLAND**
Zürich — Kunsthaus

**U.S.A.**
Berkeley — University Art Museum
Buffalo — Albright Knox Art Gallery
Chicago — The Art Institute
Cleveland — Museum of Art
Dallas — Museum of Fine Art
Des Moines — Art Center
Detroit — Institute of Arts
Minneapolis — Institute of Arts
New Haven — Yale University Art Gallery
New York — The Solomon R. Guggenheim Museum
Museum of Modern Art
Omaha — Joslyn Art Museum
Poughkeepsie — Vassar College Art Gallery
Washington — The Joseph H. Hirshhorn Museum & Sculpture Garden
Phillips Collection

**VENEZUELA**
Caracas — Museo de Arte Contemporáneo

# LIST OF WORKS

**1**
Three Studies for Figures at the Base of a Crucifixion. 1944.
Oil and pastel on cardboard,
each panel 37 × 29 in./94 × 74 cm.
The Tate Gallery, London.

**2**
Figure in a Landscape. 1945.
Oil and pastel on canvas,
57 × 50½ in./145 × 128 cm.
The Tate Gallery, London.

**3**
Figure Study I. 1945-46.
Oil on canvas,
48½ × 41½ in./123 × 105.5 cm.
Private collection, England.

**4**
Painting. 1946.
Oil and tempera on canvas,
78 × 52 in./198 × 132 cm.
The Museum of Modern Art, New York.

**5**
Head I. 1948.
Oil and tempera on cardboard,
40½ × 29½ in./103 × 75 cm.
Collection Richard S. Zeisler, New York.

**6**
Head VI. 1949.
Oil on canvas,
36¾ × 30¼ in./ 93 × 77 cm.
The Arts Council of Great Britain, London.

**7**
Head III. 1949.
Oil on canvas,
32 × 26 in./81 × 66 cm.
Private collection, Switzerland.

**8**
Study from the Human Body. 1949.
Oil on canvas,
58 × 51½ in./147.5 × 131 cm.
The National Gallery of Melbourne (Felton
Bequest).

**9**
Study for Crouching Nude. 1952.
Oil on canvas,
78 × 53⅞ in./198 × 137 cm.
The Detroit Institute of Arts (Gift of Mr. William
R. Valentiner, Detroit).

**10**
Dog. 1952.
Oil on canvas,
78¼ × 54¼ in./199 × 138 cm.
The Museum of Modern Art, New York.

**11**
Study after Velázquez's Portrait of Pope
Innocent X. 1953.
Oil on canvas,
60¼ × 46½ in./153 × 118 cm.
Des Moines Art Center, Iowa.

**12**
Man with Dog. 1953.
Oil on canvas,
60 × 46 in./152.5 × 117 cm.
Albright-Knox Art Gallery, Buffalo, N.Y.

**13**
Two Figures. 1953.
Oil on canvas,
60 × 45⅞ in./152.5 × 116.5 cm.
Private collection, England.

**14**
Three Studies of the Human Head. 1953.
Triptych.
Oil on canvas,
each panel 24 × 20 in./61 × 51 cm.
Private collection.

**15**
Study for a Portrait. 1953.
Oil on canvas,
60 × 46½ in./152 × 118 cm.
Kunsthalle, Hamburg.

**16**
Chimpanzee. 1955.
Oil on canvas,
60 × 46 in./152.5 × 117 cm.
Staatsgalerie, Stuttgart.

**17**
**Study for Figure IV.** 1956-57.
Oil on canvas,
60×46 in./152.5×117 cm.
National Gallery of South Australia, Adelaide.

**18**
**Study for Portrait of Van Gogh II.** 1957.
Oil on canvas,
78×56 in./198×142 cm.
Collection Edwin Janss, Thousand Oaks,
California.

**19**
**Study for Portrait of Van Gogh VI.** 1957.
Oil on canvas,
79³/₄×56 in./202.5×142 cm.
The Arts Council of Great Britain, London.

**20**
**Three Studies for a Crucifixion.** 1962.
Triptych.
Oil on canvas,
each panel 78×57 in./198×145 cm.
The Solomon R. Guggenheim Museum, New
York.

**21**
**Study from Innocent X.** 1962.
Oil on canvas,
78×55³/₄ in./198×141.5 cm.
Collection M. Riklis, New York.

**22**
**Figure in a room.** 1962.
Oil on canvas,
78×57 in./198×147 cm.
Galleria Galatea, Milan.

**23**
**Study for Three Heads.** 1962.
Small triptych.
Oil on canvas,
each panel 14×12 in./35.5×30.5 cm.
Collection William S. Paley, New York.

**24**
**Three Studies for Portrait of George Dyer (on
light ground).** 1964.
Small triptych.
Oil on canvas,
each panel 14×12 in./35.5×30.5 cm.
Private collection.

**25**
**Lying Figure with Hypodermic Syringe.** 1963.
Oil on canvas,
78×57 in./198×145 cm.
Private collection, New York.

**26**
**Double Portrait of Lucian Freud and Frank
Auerbach.** 1964.
Diptych.
Oil on canvas,
each panel 65×56³/₈ in./165×145 cm.
Moderna Museet, Stockholm.

**27**
**Three Figures in a Room.** 1964.
Triptych.
Oil on canvas,
each panel 78×58 in./198×147.5 cm.
Musée National d'Art Moderne, Centre Georges
Pompidou, Paris.

**28**
**Crucifixion.** 1965.
Triptych.
Oil on canvas,
each panel 78×58 in./198×147.5 cm.
Staatsgalerie Moderner Kunst, Munich.

**29**
**Study for Portrait (Isabel Rawsthorne).** 1964.
Oil on canvas,
78×58 in./198×147.5 cm.
Private collection, Milan.

**30**
**Three Studies for Portrait of Isabel
Rawsthorne.** 1965.
Small triptych.
Oil on canvas,
each panel 14×12 in./35.5×30.5 cm.
University of East Anglia, The Sainsbury
Collection, Norwich.

**31**
**Three Studies for Portrait of Lucian Freud.**
1965.
Small triptych.
Oil on canvas,
each panel 14×12 in./35.5×30.5 cm.
Private collection, London.

32
Portrait of Lucian Freud (on orange couch).
1965.
Oil on canvas,
61½ × 54¾ in./156 × 139 cm.
Private collection, Switzerland.

33
Three Studies of Isabel Rawsthorne (on white
ground). 1965.
Small triptych.
Oil on canvas,
each panel 14 × 12 in./35.5 × 30.5 cm.
Private collection, Switzerland.

34
From Muybridge — Studies of the Human Body
— Woman emptying a Bowl of Water, and
Paralytic Child on all Fours. 1965.
Oil on canvas,
78 × 58 in./198 × 147.5 cm.
Stedelijk Museum, Amsterdam.

35
Three Studies of Isabel Rawsthorne (on light
ground). 1965.
Small triptych.
Oil on canvas,
each panel 14 × 12 in./35.5 × 30.5 cm.
Private collection.

36
Three Studies of Isabel Rawsthorne. 1966.
Small triptych.
Oil on canvas,
each panel 14 × 12 in./35.5 × 30.5 cm.
Private collection, Paris.

37
Portrait of Isabel Rawsthorne. 1966.
Oil on canvas,
26¾ × 18⅛ in./67 × 46 cm.
The Tate Gallery, London.

38
Portrait of George Dyer Crouching. 1966.
Oil on canvas,
78 × 58 in./198 × 147.5 cm.
Private collection, Caracas.

39
Portrait of George Dyer Staring at Blind Cord.
1966
Oil on canvas,
78 × 58 in./198 × 147.5 cm.
Collection Maestri, Parma.

40
Three Studies for Portrait of Lucian Freud.
1966.
Triptych.
Oil on canvas,
each panel 78 × 58 in./198 × 147.5 cm.
Marlborough International Fine Art.

41
Three Studies of George Dyer. 1966.
Small triptych.
Oil on canvas,
each panel 14 × 12 in./35.5 × 30.5 cm
Private collection, New York.

42
Portrait of George Dyer Riding a Bicycle.
1966.
Oil on canvas,
78 × 58 in./198 × 147.5 cm.
Collection Jerome L. Stern, New York.

43
Three Studies of Muriel Belcher. 1966.
Small triptych.
Oil on canvas,
each panel 14 × 12 in./35.5 × 30.5 cm.
Collection James J. Shapiro, New York.

44
Portrait of George Dyer Talking. 1966.
Oil on canvas,
78 × 58 in./198 × 147.5 cm.
Private collection, New York.

45
Study of Isabel Rawsthorne. 1966.
Oil on canvas,
14 × 12 in./35.5 × 30.5 cm.
Private collection, Paris.

46
Study for Head of George Dyer and Isabel
Rawsthorne. 1967.
Diptych.
Oil on canvas,
each panel 14 × 12 in./35.5 × 30.5 cm.
Private collection, Italy.

47
Triptych inspired by T.S. Eliot's Poem
"Sweeney Agonistes". 1967.
Oil and pastel on canvas,
each panel 78 × 58 in./198 × 147.5 cm.
Hirshhorn Museum & Sculpture Garden,
Smithsonian Institution, Washington, D.C.

48
Study for Head of George Dyer. 1967.
Oil on canvas,
14 × 12 in./35.5 × 30.5 cm.
Private collection.

49
Lying Figure. 1966.
Oil on canvas,
78 × 58 in./198 × 147.5 cm.
Marlborough International Fine Art.

50
Three Studies of Isabel Rawsthorne. 1967.
Oil on canvas,
47 × 60 in./119 × 152.5 cm.
Nationalgalerie Berlin.

51
Portrait of Isabel Rawsthorne Standing in a
Street in Soho. 1967.
Oil on canvas,
78 × 58 in./198 × 147.5 cm.
Nationalgalerie Berlin.

52
Three Studies for Portrait. 1968.
Small triptych.
Oil on canvas,
each panel 14 × 12 in./35.5 × 30.5 cm.
Private collection.

53
Three Studies of Isabel Rawsthorne. 1968.
Small triptych.

Oil on canvas,
each panel 14 × 12 in./35.5 × 30.5 cm.
Private collection, Nassau.

54
Two Studies for a Portrait of George Dyer.
1968.
Oil on canvas,
78 × 58 in./198 × 147.5 cm.
Art Museum Atheneum, Helsinki, Collection Sara
Hildén.

55
Two Studies of George Dyer with Dog. 1968.
Oil on canvas,
78 × 58 in./198 × 147.5 cm.
Private collection, Rome.

56
Portrait of George Dyer in a Mirror. 1968.
Oil on canvas,
78 × 58 in./198 × 147.5 cm.
Collection H. Thyssen-Bornemisza, Lugano.

57
Two Figures Lying on a Bed with Attendants.
1968.
Triptych.
Oil and pastel on canvas,
each panel 78 × 58 in./198 × 147.5 cm.
Private collection, New York.

58
Three Studies of Henrietta Moraes. 1969.
Small triptych.
Oil on canvas,
each panel 14 × 12 in./35.5 × 30.5 cm.
Collection Gilbert de Botton, Switzerland.

59
Study of Henrietta Moraes. 1969.
Oil on canvas,
14 × 12 in./35.5 × 30.5 cm.
Private collection, Johannesburg.

60
Lying Figure. 1969.
Oil on canvas,
78 × 58 in./198 × 147.5 cm.
Private collection, Montreal.

**61**
**Study for Bullfight No. 1.** 1969.
Oil on canvas,
78×58 in./198×147.5 cm.
Private collection, Switzerland.

**62**
**Three Studies of Lucian Freud.** 1969.
Triptych.
Oil on canvas,
each panel 78×58 in./198×147.5 cm.
Private collection, Rome.

**63**
**Henrietta Moraes.** 1969.
Oil on canvas,
14×12 in./35.5×30.5 cm.
Private collection, Dublin.

**64**
**Three Studies of Henrietta Moraes.** 1969.
Small triptych.
Oil on canvas,
each panel 14×12 in./35.5×30.5 cm.
Collection Galleria Galatea, Milan.

**65**
**Three Studies of George Dyer.** 1969.
Small triptych.
Oil on canvas,
each panel 14×12 in./35.5×30.5 cm.
Collection Madame Lucie Germain, Paris.

**66**
**Study of Nude with Figure in a Mirror.** 1969.
Oil on canvas,
78×58 in./198×147.5 cm.
Marlborough International Fine Art.

**67**
**Studies of George Dyer and Isabel Rawsthorne.**
1969.
Diptych.
Oil on canvas,
each panel 14×12 in./35.5×30.5 cm.
Private collection, Switzerland.

**68**
**Self-Portrait.** 1969.
Oil on canvas,
14×12 in./35.5×30.5 cm.
Private collection, London.

**69**
**Three Studies of the Male Back.** 1970.
Triptych.
Oil on canvas,
each panel 78×58 in./198×147.5 cm.
Kunsthaus, Zürich.

**70**
**Self-Portrait.** 1970.
Oil on canvas,
59$^7/_8$×58 in./152×147.5 cm.
Private collection, London.

**71**
**Study for Portrait.** 1970.
Oil on canvas,
78×58 in./198×147.5 cm.
Private collection, France.

**72**
**Studies of the Human Body.** 1970.
Triptych.
Oil on canvas,
each panel 78×58 in./198×147.5 cm.
Marlborough International Fine Art.

**73**
**Study for Portrait.** 1971.
Oil on canvas,
78×58 in./198×147.5 cm.
Private collection, London.

**74**
**Second version of "Painting 1946".** 1971.
Oil on canvas,
78×58 in./198×147.5 cm.
Wallraf-Richartz-Museum, Ludwig Collection,
Cologne.

**75**
**Studies from the Human Body.** 1970.
Triptych.
Oil on canvas,
each panel 78×58 in./198×147.5 cm.
Private collection, Switzerland.

**76**
**Study for Portrait of Lucian Freud (Sideways).**
1971.
Oil on canvas,
78×58 in./198×147.5 cm.
Private collection, Brussels.

77
**Female Nude Standing in a Doorway.** 1972.
Oil on canvas,
78 × 58 in./198 × 147.5 cm.
Private collection, France.

78
**Three Studies for Self-Portrait.** 1972.
Small triptych.
Oil on canvas,
each panel 14 × 12 in./35.5 × 30.5 cm.
Collection Basil P. Goulandris, Lausanne.

79
**Self-Portrait.** 1971.
Oil on canvas,
14 × 12 in./35.5 × 30.5 cm.
Collection Michel Leiris, Paris.

80
**Self-Portrait.** 1972.
Oil on canvas,
14 × 12 in./35.5 × 30.5 cm.
Private collection, London.

81
**Self-Portrait with Injured Eye.** 1972.
Oil on canvas,
14 × 12 in./35.5 × 30.5 cm.
Private collection.

82
**Triptych.** 1971.
Oil on canvas,
each panel 78 × 58 in./198 × 147.5 cm.
Private collection, New York.

83
**Three Studies of Figures on Beds.** 1972.
Triptych.
Oil and pastel on canvas,
each panel 78 × 58 in./198 × 147.5 cm.
Private collection.

84
**Self-Portrait.** 1972.
Oil on canvas,
78 × 58 in./198 × 147.5 cm.
Private collection, New York.

85
**Three Studies for Self-Portrait.** 1973.
Small triptych.
Oil on canvas,
each panel 14 × 12 in./35.5 × 30.5 cm.
Private collection, Switzerland.

86
**Self-Portrait.** 1972.
Oil on canvas,
14 × 12 in./35.5 × 30.5 cm.
Collection Gilbert de Botton, Switzerland.

87
**Self-Portrait.** 1973.
Oil on canvas,
78 × 58 in./198 × 147.5 cm.
Private collection.

88
**Study for a Human Body - Man Turning on the Light.** 1973-74.
Oil on canvas,
78 × 58 in./198 × 147.5 cm.
The Royal College of Art, London.

89
**Triptych. August.** 1972.
Oil on canvas,
each panel 78 × 58 in./198 × 147.5 cm.
The Tate Gallery, London.

90
**Triptych. May-June.** 1973.
Oil on canvas,
each panel 78 × 58 in./198 × 147.5 cm.
Private collection, New York.

91
**Self-Portrait.** 1973.
Oil on canvas,
14 × 12 in./35.5 × 30.5 cm.
Private collection.

92
**Self-Portrait.** 1973.
Oil on canvas,
78 × 58 in./198 × 147.5 cm.
Collection Claude Bernard, Paris.

**93**
Sleeping Figure. 1974.
Oil on canvas,
78 × 58 in./198 × 147.5 cm.
Collection David Sylvester, London.

**94**
Seated Figure. 1974.
Oil and pastel on canvas,
78 × 58 in./198 × 147.5 cm.
Collection Gilbert de Botton, Switzerland.

**95**
Three Portraits. Posthumous Portrait of George
Dyer, Self-Portrait, Portrait of Lucian Freud.
1973.
Triptych.
Oil on canvas,
each panel 78 × 58 in./198 × 147.5 cm.
Marlborough International Fine Art.

**96**
Three Studies for Self-Portrait. 1974.
Small triptych.
Oil on canvas,
each panel 14 × 12 in./35.5 × 30.5 cm.
Collection Carlos Haime, Bogotá.

**97**
Self-Portrait. 1975.
Oil on canvas,
14 × 12 in./35.5 × 30.5 cm.
Private collection.

**98**
Portrait of a Dwarf. 1975.
Oil on canvas,
62 ½ × 23 in./158.5 × 58.5 cm.
Private collection, New South Wales.

**99**
Three Studies for Portrait of Peter Beard.
1975.
Small triptych.
Oil on canvas,
each panel 14 × 12 in./35.5 × 30.5 cm.
Private collection, Paris.

**100**
Three Studies for Portrait of Peter Beard.
June 1975.
Small triptych.

Oil on canvas,
each panel 14 × 12 in./35.5 × 30.5 cm.
Private collection, New York.

**101**
Three Figures and Portrait. 1975.
Oil and pastel on canvas,
78 × 58 in./198 × 147.5 cm.
The Tate Gallery, London.

**102**
Studies from the Human Body. 1975.
Oil on canvas,
78 × 58 in./198 × 147.5 cm.
Collection Gilbert de Botton, Switzerland.

**103**
Triptych. March. 1974.
Oil on canvas,
each panel 78 × 58 in./198 × 147.5 cm.
Private collection, Madrid.

**104**
Figure at a Washbasin. 1976.
Oil on canvas,
78 × 58 in./198 × 147.5 cm.
Museo de Arte Contemporáneo, Caracas.

**105**
Figure in Movement. 1976.
Oil on canvas,
78 × 58 in./198 × 147.5 cm.
Galerie Claude Bernard, Paris.

**106**
Three Studies for Self-Portrait. 1976.
Small triptych.
Oil on canvas,
each panel 14 × 12 in./35.5 × 30.5 cm.
Collection H. Thyssen-Bornemisza, Lugano.

**107**
Portrait of Michel Leiris. 1976.
Oil on canvas,
14 × 12 in./35.5 × 30.5 cm.
Collection Michel Leiris, Paris.

**108**
Triptych. 1974-77.
Oil and pastel on canvas,
each panel 78 × 58 in./198 × 147.5 cm.
Property of the Artist.

**109**
Triptych. 1976.
Oil and pastel on canvas,
each panel 78 × 58 in./198 × 147.5 cm.
Private collection, France.

**110**
Figure Writing Reflected in a Mirror. 1976.
Oil on canvas,
78 × 58 in./198 × 147.5 cm.
Private collection, Paris.

**111**
Two Studies for Self-Portrait. 1977.
Diptych.
Oil on canvas,
each panel 14 × 12 in./35.5 × 30.5 cm.
Private collection.

**112**
Seated Figure. 1977.
Oil on canvas,
78 × 58 in./198 × 147.5 cm.
Mrs. Susan Lloyd, Nassau.

**113**
Study for Portrait. 1977.
Oil on canvas,
78 × 58 in./198 × 147.5 cm.
Private collection, Monaco.

**114**
Self-Portrait. 1978.
Oil on canvas,
78 × 58 in./198 × 147.5 cm.
Private collection.

**115**
Two Studies for Portrait of Richard Chopping.
1978.
Diptych.
Oil on canvas,
each panel 14 × 12 in./35.5 × 30.5 cm.
Private collection, Paris.

**116**
Study for Portrait (Michel Leiris). 1978.
Oil on canvas,
14 × 12 in./35.5 × 30.5 cm.
Collection Michel Leiris, Paris.

**117**
Seated Figure. 1978.
Oil on canvas,
78 × 58 in./198 × 147.5 cm.
Private collection, Malibu.

**118**
Landscape. 1978.
Oil and pastel on canvas,
78 × 58 in./198 × 147.5 cm.
Private collection, Switzerland.

**119**
Figure in Movement. 1978.
Oil and pastel on canvas,
78 × 58 in./198 × 147.5 cm.
Private collection, Los Angeles.

**120**
Painting. 1978.
Oil on canvas,
78 × 58 in./198 × 147.5 cm.
Private collection, Monaco.

**121**
Study for Portrait. 1978.
Oil on canvas,
78 × 58 in./198 × 147.5 cm.
Private collection, Hartford, Conn.

**122**
Jet of Water. 1979.
Oil on canvas,
78 × 58 in./198 × 147.5 cm.
Private collection, New York.

**123**
Triptych - Studies of the Human Body. 1979.
Oil on canvas,
each panel 78 × 58 in./198 × 147.5 cm.
Sutton Place Heritage Trust Ltd., Guildford.

**124**
Two Seated Figures. 1979.
Oil on canvas,
78 × 58 in./198 × 147.5 cm.
Collection Dr. Theodore J. Edlich Jr.,
New York.

125
**Seated Figure.** 1979.
Oil on canvas,
78 × 58 in./198 × 147.5 cm.
Marlborough International Fine Art.

126
**Three Studies for Self-Portrait.** 1979.
Small triptych.
Oil on canvas,
each panel 14¾ × 12½ in./37.5 × 31.8 cm.
Private collection, Mexico.

127
**Sphinx - Portrait of
Muriel Belcher.** 1979.
Oil on canvas,
78 × 58 in./198 × 147.5 cm.
Property of the Artist.

128
**Three Studies for a Portrait of John Edwards.**
1980.
Small triptych.
Oil on canvas,
each panel 14 × 12 in./35.5 × 30.5 cm.
Marlborough International Fine Art.

129
**The Wrestlers, after Muybridge.** 1980.
Oil and pastel on canvas,
78 × 58 in./198 × 147.5 cm.
Private collection, Tokyo.

130
**Study for Portrait with
Bird in Flight.** 1980.
Oil on canvas,
78 × 58 in./198 × 147.5 cm.
Private collection, Toronto.

131
**Carcase of Meat and Bird of Prey.** 1980.
Oil and pastel on canvas,
78 × 58 in./198 × 147.5 cm.
Collection Claude Bernard, Paris.

132
**Study for Self-Portrait.** 1980.
Oil on canvas,
14 × 12 in./35.5 × 30.5 cm.
Sutton Place Heritage Trust Ltd., Guildford.

133
**Study of a Man Talking.** 1981.
Oil on canvas,
78 × 58 in./198 × 147.5 cm.
Private collection, Berne.

134
**Triptych.** 1981.
Inspired by the Oresteia of Aeschylus.
Oil on canvas,
each panel 78 × 58 in./198 × 147.5 cm.
Marlborough International Fine Art.

135
**Study for Portrait.** 1981.
Oil on canvas,
78 × 58 in./198 × 147.5 cm.
Marlborough International Fine Art.

136
**Sand Dune.** 1981.
Oil and pastel on canvas,
78 × 58 in./198 × 147.5 cm.
Marlborough International Fine Art.

137
**Study for Self-Portrait.** 1981.
Oil on canvas,
78 × 58 in./198 × 147.5 cm.
Von der Heydt Museum, Wuppertal.

138
**Study from the Human Body.** 1981.
Oil on canvas,
78 × 58 in./198 × 147.5 cm.
Property of the Artist.

139
**Study of the Human Body.** 1982.
Oil and pastel on canvas,
78 × 58 in./198 × 147.5 cm.
Musée National d'Art Moderne, Centre Georges
Pompidou, Paris.

140
**Study of the Human Body
from a Drawing by Ingres.** 1982.
Oil and pastel on canvas,
78 × 58 in./198 × 147.5 cm.
Property of the Artist.

**141**

**Water from a Running Tap.** 1982.
Oil on canvas,
78 × 58 in./198 × 147.5 cm.
Private collection, Madrid.

**142**

**Three Studies for Portrait (Mick Jagger).** 1982.
Small triptych.
Oil and pastel on canvas,
each panel 14 × 12 in./35.5 × 30.5 cm.
Private collection, New York.

**143**

**Study for Self-Portrait.** 1982.
Oil on canvas,
78 × 58 in./198 × 147.5 cm.
Private collection, New York.

**144**

**Study of the Human Body. Figure in Movement.** 1982.
Oil on canvas,
78 × 58 in./198 × 147.5 cm.
Marlborough International Fine Art.

**145**

**A Piece of Waste Land.** 1982.
Oil on canvas,
78 × 58 in./198 × 147.5 cm.
Property of the Artist.

**146**

**Study of the Human Body.** 1983.
Oil and pastel on canvas,
78 × 58 in./198 × 147.5 cm.
Property of the Artist.